Tokelau Science Education and Research Program: Atafu Fieldwork August 2008

by
David J. Addison
John Kalolo

A joint publication of:
The Tokelau Department of Education and
The Samoan Studies Institute, American Samoa Community College

Polokalame Akoakoga Faka Haienihi i Tokelau: Galuega Faka Tino i Atafu 2008

tuhia
David J. Addison
John Kalolo

Kua mafai ke fai tenei tuhi ona ko te galulue fakatahi o
te Mataeke o Akoakoga a Tokelau fakatahi ai ma
te Mataeke fakapatino kina matakupu Samoa mai
American Samoan Community College.

photo: Timothy Gallaher

Cover photos by Timothy Gallaher
Book design by Robin Stephen: www.vitzys.com

Published by:

Samoan Studies Institute
American Samoa Community College
Pago Pago, AS 96799
USA

and

Tokelau Department of Education
Atafu
Tokelau Islands

ISBN 978-0-9818524-2-3

photos: Timothy Gallaher

ACKNOWLEDGEMENTS

Our warmest thanks go to the Nuku of Atafu, the Taupulega o Atafu, the Fatupaepae o Atafu, and the Aumaga o Atafu for making this project happen. We thank them all for their support and for welcoming the off-island team members so wholeheartedly to Atafu.

The USP Atafu Satellite Campus, Matauala School, and the Taupulega staff gave us much needed logistical and moral support.

The off-island team members would not have arrived in Tokelau on time without transportation from Anne and Barry Lange of "Cat's Paw IV" and Gail and David Funk of "5th Season". They bravely stayed on and helped with the archaeological survey – we wish they could have stayed longer.

Lameka and Louisa and Asora and Faailoa graciously opened their homes for accommodation of off-island team members. Many families provided us with food, invited us into their homes for meals and befriended the off-island team members in many ways. We can't thank the people of Atafu enough for making us truly feel like "part of the family".

The 2008 research was partially funded by a grant from the University of the South Pacific, to whom we are grateful. We thank Chair Randy Baker and the ASCC Social Sciences Department for contribut-ing to student travel expenses. Director Okenasia Manila-Fauolo and the ASCC Samoan Studies Insti-tute have contributed in ways too numerous to mention.

Photographs were graciously provided by Tony Atoni, Timali Pele, David Funk, Bryon Bass, Rintaro Ono, Timothy Gallaher, Adam Thompson, and Hilary Scotthorn.

FAKAFETAI FAKAPITOA

Muamua e fakafetai lahi lele kite kauafua tena i Atafu, ki te Taupulega o Atafu, te Fatupaepae ma te Aumaga na mafai ai ke fakatino tenei polokalame. E fakafetai atu ki tagata uma o Atafu kite lagolago ma te fakafeiloaki atu kite kau malaga.

Na lahi lele te fehoahoani na maua mai foki, mai te USP i Atafu, fakatahi ai mai te aoga a Matauala ma te kau tautua a te Taupulega o Atafu.

E talitonu kana he momoli atu kimatou e Anne ma Barry Lange ite vaka faila teia e takua ko te "Cat's Paw IV", fakatahi ai ma te vaka faila teia e takua kote "5th Season" o Gail ma David Funk na tuai atu te kau Malaga ki Atafu. Na lahi foki he hao ma ni taumafaiga a na uho ienei i na galuega na fakatino i Atafu, nae momoko lele ke mafai ke loa he tatou mafutaga.

Na fakaavanoa mai foki na maota o na matua kia Loiusa ma Lameka Sale fakatahi ai ma na matua kia Faailoa ma Asora Tonuia, ke nonofo ai te kau Malaga. Na lahi lele a matou meakai na maua mai i na kaiga, kimatou foki na lahi faka afe e na kaiga ke fai he matou katamuga, pe omomoe kimatou. E he lava ni kupu e mafai ke tuku atu kina tino o Atafu, mo te tauhiga ma te foki mai ote lagona ko kimatou e i loto o tenei kaiga.

E momoli foki te fakafetai ki na vaega tupe na fehoahoani mai ai te Iunivehite ote Pahefika i Saute (USP), mo te fakatinoga o tenei polokalame mo te 2008.

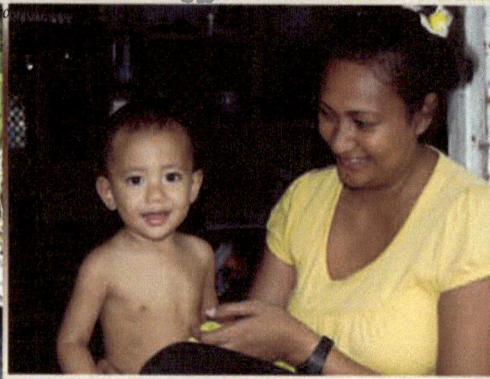

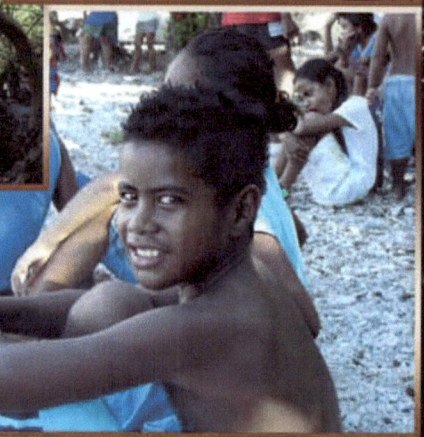

photos: Timothy Gallaher and Bryon Bass

DEDICATION

We dedicate our work to the past generations of Tokelau whose spirit we hope to be worthy of carrying forward and to the Lumanaki o Tokelau, in whose hands the future of Tokelau rests.

ALOFAAGA

E momoli oko ienei taumafaiga kina augatupulaga teia kua momoe atu, ma te fakamoemoe ke aoga na taumafaiga mo kilatou, fakatahi ai mo te lumanaki o Tokelau, aua kua i olatou lima te lumanaki o Tokelau.

photo: Bryon Bass

photos: Timothy Gallaher

photo: Timothy Gallaher

WHY SCIENCE FOR TOKELAU?

Tokelau has a strong oral history documenting many aspects of the past. We cherish this record and in no way do we want to minimize it or neglect it's importance. Also, we are not the experts in this area, and we know that the elders who are the keepers of this knowledge are the proper authorities to talk about it. We humbly hope that whatever understandings we can contribute from science will contribute to enriching Tokelau's existing knowledge systems.

Tokelau has a long history of sustainable resource management. This has allowed the people of Tokelau to create and maintain a vibrant culture in an atoll environment with limited natural resources. Modernity and integration with the world economy means that Tokelau is now involved in issues ranging far beyond its borders.

Like the rest of the world, many of the challenges facing Tokelau in the 21st century will have solutions based in science (e.g., waste management; water quality;

KO HEA TE MANAKOMIA AI TE HAIENIHI MO TOKELAU?

Ko Tokelau e lahi lele ona tala tuku e fakamaumau ai ona tala fakaholopito. E taua lele na fakamuamuaga ienei kia te kimatou, ma kitea e kimatou tona taua. Ko kimatou foki, e he ni tino e popoto i na vaega ienei, e kimatou iloa ko na tino matutua, na tino e taofia e kilatou te iloa tenei, ko na tino ia e patino ma tatau ke tautatala ki na vaega ienei. E fakamoemoe ma te loto maualalo, ko hea lava he hao mo te haienihi, e lahi hona hao kite fakalauiatelega ona iloa mo Tokelau agai ki ona tala fakaholopito.

Ko te pulepulega o na lihohi a Tokelau kohe mea kua leva. Te iloa tenei na mafai ai e Tokelau oi fakaauau ai ana nofononofoga i he hikomaga e he lahi ai ni lihohi. Ko te lahi o te hokotaga ki ietahi nuku kua kitea ai foki te lahi oni vaega pe ni matakupu e he mahani ai ia Tokelau.

E ve lava ko te tulaga kua iei ai te lalolagi katoa, te lahiga o na lukitau e fakafegai ma Tokelau i te 21 Senituli e maua mai ni ona fofo i na matakupu faka haienihi.Ko ni fakatakitakiga, ko te iloa oi

coral bleaching and reef health; fish stock management; food security; global climate change; sea-level rise; erosion; storm mitigation; etc.). The time is now to start planning to enhance the knowledge and skills that have served Tokelau well for centuries. Scientific knowledge will be increasingly important to Tokelau in coming years.

As Tokelau decision makers confront the challenges of the coming decades, it is critically important to have scientific knowledge and perspectives available. Although outside science consultants can be used, the most effective way is having Tokelau's sons and daughters trained in sciences.

This project will begin training young Tokelauans in science so that they will be available in the future to enhance Tokelau's unique system of local consensus-based decision making. Internationally, local capacity building is seen as a highly effective and efficient use of development funds to achieve long-term change.

The process of becoming a trained scientist takes many years (for example BA=4 years; MA 2-3 years more; PhD 4-6 years more). Thus, it is critical to begin Tokelau youth in the process immediately. Every year of delay adds a year to the time when sons and daughters of Tokelau will be fully trained scientists available to assist the community.

The most effective way to interest students in science

kikila fakalelei te faiga ona otaota pe ko na lapihi, te kikilaga fakalelei o te huavai taumafa, te kikilaga o te lau akau, te pulepulega o na lihohi o te tai, ko te kikilaga o na meakai, ko te malamalama ki te huiga o te tau, ko te huiga kite tai, ko te tokehea pe ko tafea o te laukelekele, ma ie tahi mea. Ko te taimi nei kua taua lele ke kamata peleni ke fakalautele te iloa teia kua leva te fakaaoga e Tokelau, ite fia senituli. E taua lahi lele ke maua te tomai faka Haienihi mo Tokelau mo tona lumanaki.

E lahi lele na fakafitauli e faka feagai mo tagata fai tonu mo Tokelau i na tauhaga i mua, teia e taua ai ke maua ni iloa faka haienihi. Atonu e mafai ke fakaaoga e kitatou na iloa mai fafo, kae e hili atu te holoholo manuia ma taunuku ienei vaega kafai e fai lava e ni tama fanau a Tokelau kua uma te koleni i na vaega faka haienihi.

Ko tenei polokalame, kua kamata koleni ai ia tama fanau a Tokelau, kae ke fehoahoani kilatou i na tonu fai. i na nuku i fafo, e lahi lele te taua ote fakaaoga ona tupe atiake ohe nuku kini polokalame e fakalautele ai te mafai ma te iloa o tagata.

E lahi na tauhaga e koleni ai he tino ke lava hona tomai ina matakupu faka haienihi, fakatakitakiga: kote BA, 4 tauhaga; kote MA, 2-3 tauhaga; kote PhD, 4-6 tauhaga pe hili atu. Te ia e taua ai ke kamata loa oi koleni ia tupulaga o Tokelau. Ko te fai mea tuku o kitatou, ko he tauhaga foki tena kua tuai maua ai loa ni tamaiti pe ni tama fanau a Tokelau, ke fehoahoani ki na nuku ma te atunuku.

photo: Timothy Gallaher

careers is to involve them directly in research. In collaboration with the Tokelau Department of Education and USP Tokelau, this project will bring professional research scientists to each atoll in Tokelau. Students will be incorporated into research-based "learning groups" where they will be thrilled with the excitement of direct scientific inquiry.

The research the students participate in will begin building basic scientific knowledge about Tokelau. The students will be encouraged to attend the universities that the participating scientists come from. As the students begin their path of scientific education at these universities, the scientists will be there to help guide them on their paths.

When students reach a certain level, they will be able to continue research in Tokelau, first under the mentorship of their scientist-partners and later as fully formed independent researchers. In this way, they will be part of a continuing program of scientific research in Tokelau. About a decade after initiation of the program, Tokelau's own scientists will be the ones driving scientific research in Tokelau and advising decision makers on scientific topics.

Although it will take a decade to produce fully trained Tokelauan scientists, the community benefits

Ko te auala e mafai ke taunuku ai ienei taumafaiga, pe mafai ke fiafia ai te tamaiti ki na matakupu faka haienihi, ko te tuku o kilatou kini polokalame hukehuke, e lahi tagolima ai te tamaiti kina galuega fakatino. Kua galulue fakatahi kimatou ma te Mataeke o Akoakoga a Tokelau ,fakatahi ai ma te Iunivehite o te Pahefika i Saute ke kaumai ni tino kua lahi to latou tomai i na matakupu faka haienihi ki na motu o Tokelau.

Ko tamaiti aoga e tuku kini kulupu e galuelue ai, ma fakatino e kilatou ni polokalame faka haienihi, ke maua e kilatou te inatalehi pe ko te fiafia ki ienei matakupu.

Ko te hukehukega e fakatino e na tamaiti, e kamata maua ai e te tamaiti he iloa faka haienihi agai ki Tokelau. E taumafai foki ke fautuagia ieni fanau ke aoga ina Iunivehite e mautu ma faiaoga ai na haienitihi ,pe ko na tino kua ia te kilatou te iloa fakapitoa i na matakupu faka haienihi. E taua lele aua e mafai na haienitihi ienei ke fehoahoani ma foki he takiala mo te tamaiti i te taimi kua aoga ai ina Iunivehite i fafo.

E iei te taimi e mafai ai te tamaiti ke hau fai hana hukehukega fakatahi ma na haienitihi e faufautua ki ei, kae i he taimi i mua, kua mafai lava oi fakatino na hukehukega e ia. Ko te agaga e tatia ai ni fuafuaga venei, e kitea ai he auala e faigofie ma lava he fehoahoani e kave ki na fanau, ma kitea ai foki ko te polokalame e fakaauau pea. Ke maua ai ni haienitihi Tokelau e fakatino e kilatou na hukehukega e fai i Tokelau, ma faufautua kini fakafitauli faka haienihi ki na tino fai tonu mo Tokelau.

will be immediate. During the project field-research seasons, the visiting scientists will give community informational meeting on various aspects of science. The students will also be guided in preparing their own presentations to the community – showing what they have learned at each stage. These community meetings will begin a process of raising scientific awareness and knowledge level among the whole population in Tokelau communities.

This capacity-building science educational and research project will have profound benefits on Tokelau. It will begin effecting the community immediately but the effects will last for generations to come.

TOKELAU SCIENCE EDUCATION AND RESEARCH PROGRAM (2008-2011)

This is a multidisciplinary and international project in cooperation with the Tokelau Department of Education and University of the South Pacific (USP), Tokelau. The project co-directors are David Addison (American Samoa Community College) and John Kalolo (Tokelau Department of Education).

Atonu e maua he sefulu tauhaga ke maua ai ni haienitihi Tokelau, kako te aoga o te polokalame mo na nuku e iloga lava i te taimi kua fakatino ai te polokalame. i te taimi e fakatino ai tenei polokalame e lahi lele ni vaega e tuku atu e te kau malaga pe ko na haienitihi i ni mafutaga fakatahi ma te nuku. i na mafutaga fakatahi ma te nuku, e kave foki te avanoa ki na fanau ke fakamatala mai a latou galuega kua fakatino.Ko na mafutaga la ienei kua kamata tuku atu ai te iloa faka haienihi ki tagata o te nuku, kae ke hikitia ma fakalauitele te iloa faka haienihi ki tagata uma o Tokelau.

Ko te polokalame akoako tenei mo te fakalauaitelega o te iloa faka haienihi e lahi lele tona taua mo Tokelau. Ko na leleiga ienei e iloga lava ma kitea, i te taimi e kamata ai te polokalame, ma fakaauau atu lava ki na tupuluga koi mua.

POLOKALAME HUKEHUKE FAKA HAIENIHI I TOKELAU (2008-2011)

Ko te polokalam tenei e galulue fakatahi ma te Mataeke o Akoakoga o Tokelau, fakatahi ma te Iunivehite ote Pahefika i Saute (USP) i Tokelau. Ko te polokalame tenei kua faka foe e David Addison (American Samoa Community College) ma John Kalolo (Matauala School Tokelau).

photo: Timali Pele

photo: David Addison

PROJECT GENERAL DESCRIPTION

The project will bring a group of 15 scientists and specialists and 10 Samoan university students to each atoll in Tokelau for one month per year. They will do primary research on Tokelau based on a theme of "1000 Years of Sustainable Resource Management". Three main goals are seen as having effects over different time periods:

1. Community science education (short term)

This will target the whole population and raise awareness about various aspects of science focusing on natural sciences and human ecology. The main vehicle will be public meetings with PowerPoint presentations on focused topics followed by community discussions. As well as a basic set of presentations, topics will be chosen dependent on the communities' perceived needs for specific scientific knowledge (e.g., community meetings on Atafu in April 2008 suggest wide interest in a better understanding of Global Climate Change). Because of Tokelau's participatory and consensus based decision making, it is important to have an informed population as communities face the challenges of the 21st Century.

FAKAMATALAGA AGAI KITE POLOKALAME

E toka 15 ia haienitihi ma ni tamaiti aoga Samoa e toka 10 e aoga i te Iunivehite i Amelika Samoa e malaga atu ki na motu o Tokelau faka fokotahi i te tauhaga mo he mahina. E fai a latou huke-hukega agai kite pulepulega o na lihohi a Tokelau mai te 1000 tauhaga kua teka atu. E tolu ia vaega e kautu ki ei tenei polokalame, e tino mai ini piliota kehekehe.

1. Akoakoga faka Haienihi mo te nuku (piliota pili mai)

Ko te vaega muamua tenei, ko te tuku atu pe taumafai ke hiki-tia ma fakalauaitele te iloa o te nuku ki na matakupu fakahaienihi. E mafai ke tino tenei vaega, i ni mafutaga fakatahi ma te nuku, e mafai ai ke fai ni matakupu ke talatalanoa ai ma te nuku. E he gata i na matakupu e tuku atu ki te nuku, kae e filifili foki ni matakupu e fia malamalama atili ki ei na nuku. Fakatakitakiga, kote mafutaga ma Atafu i Apelila 2008, na matau ai te toka lahi o tagata nae fia malamalama atili kina matakupu agai kite hikitia o te tai. Ona kona nofonofoga o Tokelau e manakomia te leo o tagata uma, e kitea ai te taua lahi o te tuku atu o te iloa ki tagata uma mo te agai atu kina tonu fai mo na fakafitauli e fakafeagai ma Tokelau i te 21 Senituli.

2. Written and film records (medium term)

The project will result in two volumes of research results for each island; one in English aimed at a professional audience and the other in Tokelauan aimed at a popular audience. These will be available in both hardcopy and digital forms. WWW access will ensure broad availability to both academics and overseas Tokelauans. Results will also be published in academic journals. A film documentary of the project will be made.

3. Tokelauan scientists (long term)

USP Tokelau students will participate in the research. Each scientists will lead a "learning group" with a Samoan university student and several USP students. The learning group will conduct field research while at the same time learning about scientific research methods. The Samoan students will serve as role models and peer mentors for the Tokelauan students. The aim of this goal is to intrigue Tokelau students with the excitement of research. They will be encouraged to aspire to graduate studies in the sciences so that in about a decade there will be fully trained Tokelauan scientists available to serve their island communities. This will ensure an intergenerational continuation of the education and research initiated by this project. It is hoped that students will form special bonds with the scientists and may consider adopting one of them as a mentor and studying at their institution. Funding will be sought to support the Tokelau students at university.

2. Tuhituhiga ma na ata puke (piliota i lototonu)

Ko tenei polokalame e iei na tuhituhiga e fakamaumau ai na vaega na fakatino, e iei te kopi Igilihi mo tagata i fafo, fakatahi ai ma te kopi Tokelau. E maua uma na fakamaumauga ienei i ni tuhi fakatahi ai i luga ona komipiuta. i te initaneti e tuku foki ki ei na fakamaumauga ienei kae ke mafai ke maua ai na tala e na tino hukehuke i fafo fakatahi ai ma tama fanau kua aumau na nonofo i nuku i fafo. Ko na tala foki e maua mai ina hukehukega e tuhituhi ke mafai ke fakaaoga i na aoga ma na tino hukehuke. E iei foki te fakamoemoe ke puke ni ata o te polokalame tenei.

3. Haienitihi mo Tokelau (piliota mulimuli)

E fakatahi atu ma galulue na tamaiti akoga o te USP i na hukehukega. E takitaki e na haienitihi mai fafo na kulupu e tuku atu kiei na tamaiti. i na kulupu ie nei, e iei foki ma na tamaiti akoga o Samoa. Ko na kulupu ienei, e fakatino e kilatou na galuega ma maua e kilatou te tomai agai kina metotia e fakaaoga kina hukehukega faka haienihi.Ko na tamaiti Samoa i na kulupu e fehoahoani kina tamaiti ote USP i te taimi e fakatino ai ienei galuega.Ko te agaga, ko te taumafai ke foki te agaga initalehi ke fiafia na fanau kina matakupu venei. E foki kiei he lagona ke fakaauau ana taumafaiga i na matakupu faka haienihi, mo te fakamoemoe i te sefulu tauhaga i mua, kua kavea kilatou ma haienitihi e tautua mo Tokelau. E taua lele foki, ke kitea ai te fakauaau o na akoakoga o tama fanau a Tokelau kua auala atu i tenei polokalame. E fakamoemoe e maua he mafutaga lelei a na fanau ma na haienitihi, kae ke kavea na haienitihi ienei ma faiaoga e faka foe e ia na fanau kafai e olo kina Iunivehite e faiaoga ai na Haienitihi. E hakili foki ni fakatupega e fehoahoani kina tama fanau ienei e maua ki na Iunivehite i fafo.

photo: Rintaro Ono

photo: David Addison

ANTICIPATED PROJECT SCHEDULE

Each year will see the team on one island for one month (June-July). We will aim for completion of analyses by December, with write-up, editing and publication of results volumes by the beginning of the following field season.

2008 – pilot project on Atafu
2009 – full project on Atafu
2010 – full project on Nukunonu or Fakaofo
2011 – full project on Nukunonu or Fakaofo

TE POLOKALAME KUA FAKAMOE MOE KI EI

I tauhaga takitahi e mafuta ai te kaumalaga ma he motu e fokotahi mo he mahina(Iuni-Iulai). E fakamoemoe e totoka na galuega i te mahina o Tehema, kae ke mafai ke kamata oi tuhituhi, ma fai na vaega na maua mai ki loto o ni tuhi mo te tauhaga fou.

2008 - Tama galuega kamata i Atafu
2009 - Fakatino te polokalame uma i Atafu
2010 - Fakatino te polokalame uma i Nukunonu pe ko Fakaofo
2011 - Fakatino te polokalame uma i Nukunonu pe ko Fakaofo

photo: Timothy Galloher

RESEARCH TOPICS

The overall theme of "1000 Years of Sustainable Resource Management" will be investigated using a combination of techniques from various scientific disciplines. The following sections outline the main topics.

WHEN DID THE TOKELAU ISLANDS FORM?

The first very basic question to answer is "what is the history of sea-level changes in Tokelau". Scientific evidence has shown that over the history of the earth, sea level has gone up and down many times.

Everyone in the world is now talking about Global Climate Change (GCG) and the fact that the earth's climate is getting warmer. This means that ice at the north and south poles is melting and this raises the level of the ocean around the world.

But most people do not know that about 8500 years ago the Pacific Ocean was more than 10 metres LOWER than today. But about 4000-2000 years ago the ocean was 1.0-2.4 metres HIGHER than it is now. Scientists call this the "Mid-Holocene Highstand" (Holocene is the time the end of the last Ice Age until now, about the last 10,000 years).

NA TOPIKI PE KO NA MATAKUPU E HUKEHUKE KI EI

Ko te lautelega o te vaega e fia kikila ki ei, ko te pulepulega o na lihohi mai te 1000 tauhaga kua teka. E fakaaoga foki la ni metotia mai na vaega kehekehe ina matakupu faka haienihi ke kikila ki ei. Ko te vaega e hohoko e foki mai ai ni tahi matakupu taua.

KO ANA FEA TENA OLA AKE AI PE FAU AI NA FENUA O TOKELAU?

E venei ko te fehili faigofie muamua e tatau ke tali, "pe vefea ni tala faka holo pito agai kite hui o te tulaga kua iei te levolo ote tai i Tokelau". I na fakamaumauga faka haienihi i na tala faka holopito o te lalolagi, ko te levolo o te tai nae mahani hui. E veia e mahani fano ki luga ma fano ki lalo, e tahuihui vena.

I te taimi nei ko tagata uma o te lalolagi kua talatalanoa ki tenei matakupu, ki te hui o te tau, kite lalolagi kua fano lava e vevela pe mafanafana foki. Ko tona uiga la, ko na aiha i na Pole i Saute ma Matu kua kamata oi liu, ma kua hikitia ai te levolo ote tai ite lalolagi.

Kae kote tokalahiga o tagata e he kilatou iloa, mai te 8500 tauhaga te ia kua teka, nae katoa te 10 mita e maualalo ai te tai ite moana ote Pahefika. Kae ite 4000-2000 tauhaga kua teka atu nae katoa 1.0-2.4 mita e maualuga ai te tai o te Pahefika mai te levolo

Sea level did not come down all at one time across the Pacific. To the west of Tokelau, evidence from Funafuti Atoll in Tuvalu suggests that dryland appeared there at about 900 years ago. To the north, in the Phoenix Islands and to the east of Tokelau in the Cook Islands dry land appeared about 1100 years ago.

In Tokelau, we don't know when the sea level came down to the modern level. This is a very important question, because the motus would have been covered in water before this time. It would have been impossible for people to live in Tokelau before the sea level came down to its current level.

kua iei nei. Ko te vaega tenei e takua e na Haienitihi kote "Mid Holocene Highstand". (Ko te Holocene, ko te fakaikuga o te piliota teia e takua kote Ice Age, pe ko te 10,000 tauhaga kua teka).

Ko te huiga kite levolo ote tai e heki aofia katoa ai na koga ote Pahefika. Ki te itu i Sisifo o Tokelau, e ienei na vaega kua maua mai ite fenua o Funafuti i Tuvalu e fakamaonia ai. Ko te laukelekele matutu pe ko te fenua o Funafuti i Tuvalu na kamata hula ake pe ko te 900 tauhaga kua teka atu. Ki te agai atu kite matu o Tokelau ki Phoenix Islands, ma te agai atu ki sasae o Tokelau ki Cook Islands na hula ona fenua ite 1100 tauhaga kua teka atu.

photo: David Addison

We are fortunate that the Tokelau Science Education and Research Program included the world's foremost scientist studying the question of sealevel changes on Pacific atolls. Professor William Dickinson will examine each atoll in Tokelau and select coral samples that can be used to date sealevel change in Tokelau. Did Tokelau have dry land earlier like Tuvalu? Or later like the Cook Islands? Or was it in between?

By studying each atoll, we will also be able to see if there are differences between them. Did Fakaofo, Nukunonu and Atafu all have dry land all at the same time? Or was one atoll available for human settlement before the others?

I Tokelau, e he mautinoa pe ko ana fea tena hui mai ai te levolo o te tai ki te levolo teia kua iei nei. Ko he fehili taua tenei, aua ko na fenua venei koi lalo ai ite tai ite taimi tenei. E talitonu e he mafai ona nonofo ni tino i Tokelau, kako heki hui te levolo ote tai kite levolo teia kua iei ite taimi nei.

E fakafetai foki kitatou ona foki ko te polokalame tenei kua kaufakatahi mai ai te tahi Haienitihi o te lalolagi e pito hili ona lahi ana hukehukega agai kite huiga o te tai i te Pahefika. Kote tamana Polofesa kia William Dickinson e fakamoemoe e hukehuke uma e ia na motu o Tokelau, ma fakaoga e ia ni vaega o te lau akau ke maua mai ai ni famatalaga agai kite huiga ote levolo ote tai i Tokelau. E mafai ai ke tali na itukaiga fehili veia.Nae iei nei ni fenua pe ni laukelekele matutu i te piliota na hula ai ia Tuvalu? Pei tua mai ite taimi na hula ai na fenua o Cook Islands? Pe he piliota i te va o te tokalua tenei?

Ki te hukehuke atu kina motu takitahitahi e kitea ai foki e kitatou pe iei he kehekehega i na motu o Tokelau. Na hula uma na motu o Fakaofo, Nukunonu, ma Atafu i te taimi e fokotahi? Pe nae avanoa oi oti he fenua e fokotahi ke nofoia e tagata, oi kamata ai holo ki na tahi fenua?

photo: Tony Atoni

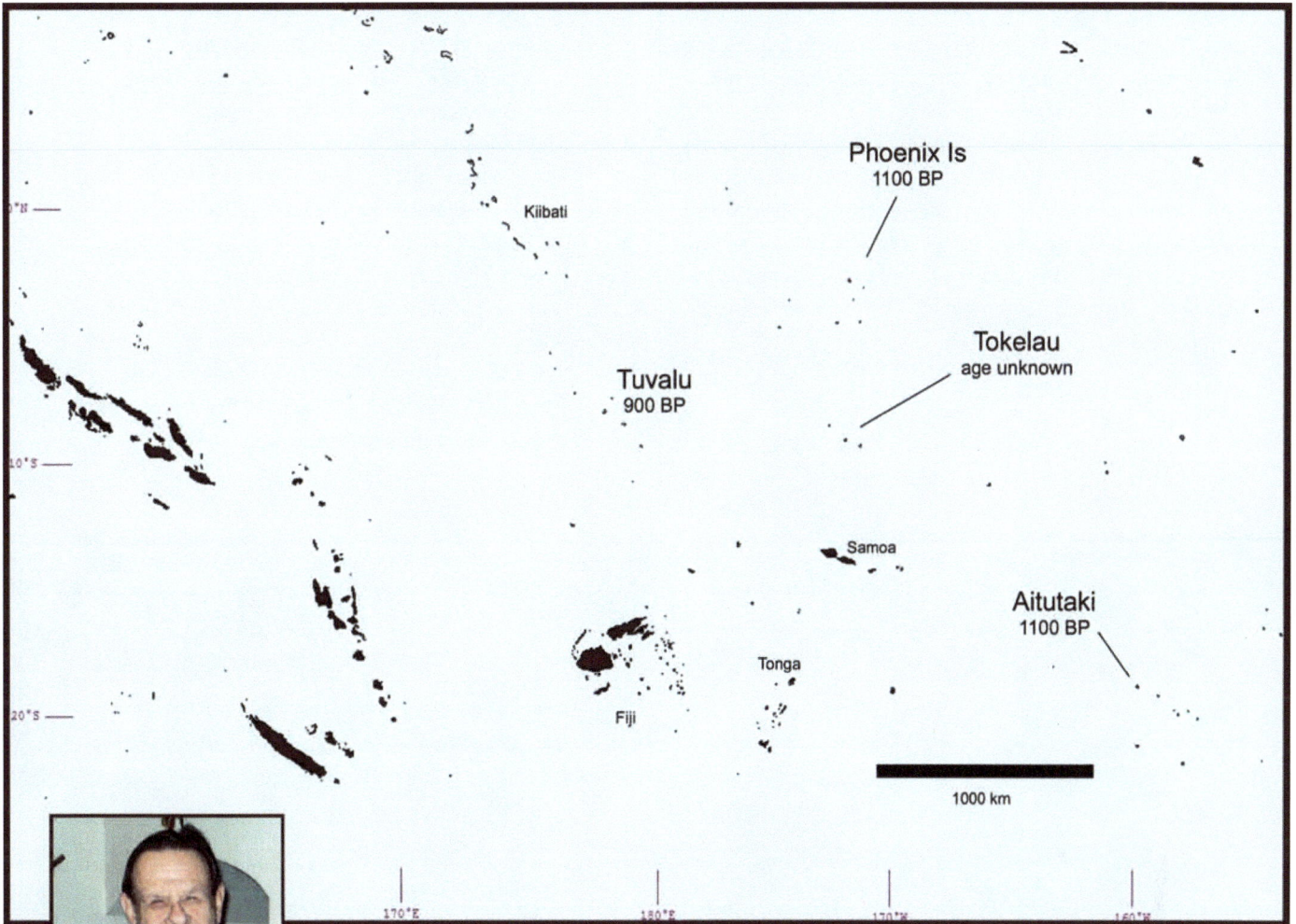

This map shows the islands surrounding Tokelau and some of the dates when dry land emerged after the Mid-Holocene Highstand. Base map courtesy of Peter Minton (http://www.evs-islands.blogspot.com).

ARCHAEOLOGY AND STRATIGRAPHY

A key concept in archaeology is that of "stratigraphy". Stratigraphy refers to the layers of soil that build up over time. The result is that the newest layers are on the top and the layers get older as you go down. Hence, the very oldest layers are at the bottom.

Archaeologist look for cultural material in the layers (things made by or discarded by humans – like broken tools or food rubbish). When there are no more layers with cultural material, we know we have reached a layer before humans started living in that place. So the deepest layer with cultural material is the layer left by the first people living in that spot.

AKELOHI MA LALO O TE LAUKELEKELE

Ko te tahi vaega taua lahi i te matakupu tenei ko te Akelohi ko te kikila kina koga kehekehe i lalo ote laukelekele. Ko na koga i luga ko ni vaega i mua mai, pe ni koga e heki leva atu. Kae kafai lava koe e agai ki lalo ko te mataloa foki ia o na koga i te laukelekele. Fakatakitakiga e hili atu te mataloa o te koga laukelekele i lalo i lo na koga laukelekele e lata ake ki luga.

Ko na tino hukehuke i tenei matakupu e kikila kini vaega nae fakaaoga i lalo o na koga kehekehe ote laukelekele, fakatakitakiga ko ni mea na fai e ni tino pe na tiaki e ni tino, veia koni mea faigaluega pe ni meakai. Kafai la e tau atu ki he koga i lalo ote lau kelekele e he toe maua ai ni mea, e kitatou iloa ko kitatou kua tau kite koga kelekele nae heai ai ni tino nae nonofo muamua ai. Tona uiga la kote koga mulimuli e toe mau ai ni mea na fai pe na tiaki e ni tino, ko te koga kelekele tena na nofoia e na tino mua-mua ote fenua, e heai ni tino i tua atu o na tino ienei.

photo: Rintaro Ono

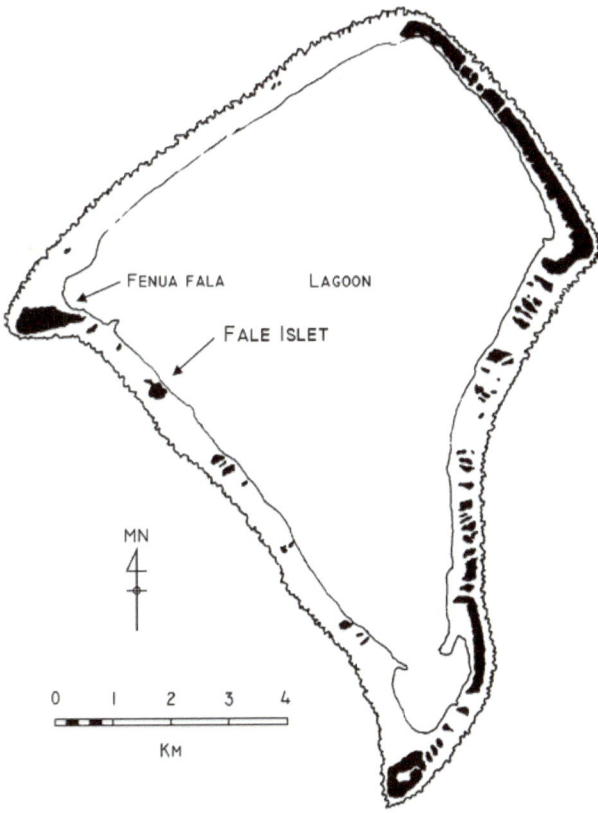

Above: Fakaofo Atoll. Courtesy of Simon Best and Andrew McAlister.

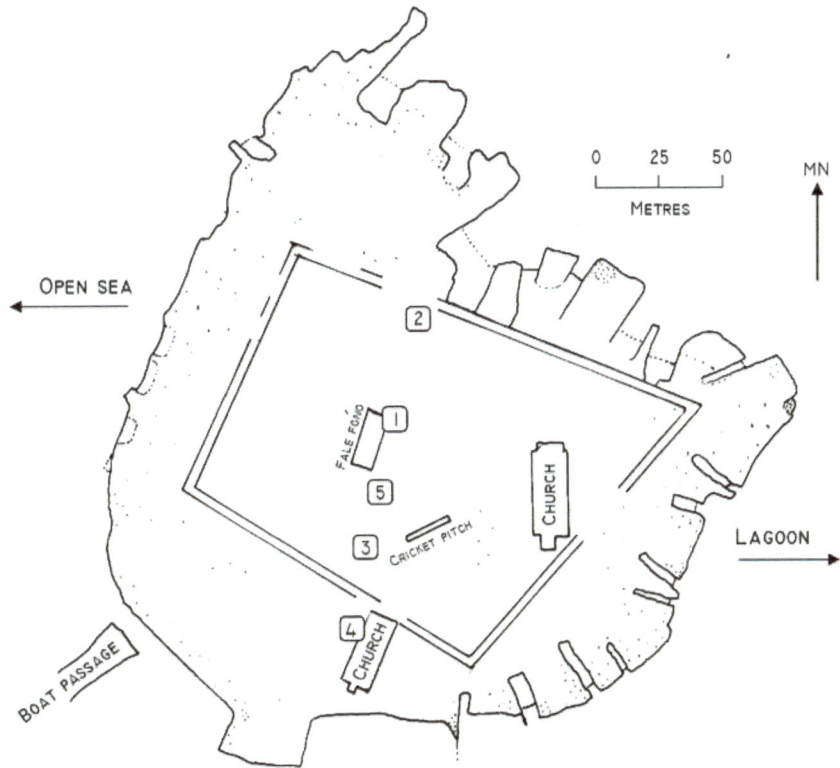

Above: Fale Islet showing locations Simon Best excavated. Courtesy of Simon Best and Andrew McAlister.

WHEN DID PEOPLE FIRST ARRIVE IN TOKELAU?

One thing that archaeology can do is find dates for things that happened in the past. But the process is not easy and there are lots of complications. The main way that archaeologists find dates is by radiocarbon dating. This can be done with anything that was living in the past. So, any kind of plant material (especially charcoal), shell, bone, and coral make good samples.

It is important to understand that radiocarbon dates always come as a range of dates. We can never find the exact year of something. The best we can do is know that the event happened at sometime in the date range. But it is hard to know if the real event was at the beginning of the range, or in the middle, or at the end.

In 1986 a New Zealand archaeologist named Simon Best did research in Tokelau. He worked mostly on Fakaofo and Atafu, with a small amount on Nukunonu.

Simon Best took radiocarbon dates from Fakaofo. He excavated near the Catholic Church. Simon found many layers of cultural material showing the lives of Fakaofo people in the past. At the very bottom he found the remains of people's food – turtle bone. A sample of the turtle bone (NZ4739) was dated with radiocarbon dating techniques.

KO ANA FEA TE NA TAUNUKU MUAMUA MAI AI NA TINO KI TOKELAU?

Ko te tahi vaega o tenei matakupu ko te hakili o na tauhaga o na mea nae tutupu i na aho kua leva. Ko te galuega tenei e he faigofie, e lahi lele na vaega kehekehe, kae ko te metotia e lahi fakaaoga e na tino Akelohi e takua ko te "radiocarbon dating". Ko te metotia tenei e mafai ke fakaaoga ki ho he mea nae ola i na aho kua leva, e veia kona lakau, pogaivi, ma te lau akau.

E tatau ke manatua e kitatou ko tenei metotia e he foki mai e ia he tauhaga e fokotahi, kae e foki mai e ia ni tauhaga e lua pe fia lava. Fakatakitakiga kafai, e lea mai ko he mea na tutupu ite 1000 kite 1002 tauhaga kua teka, e he mautinoa tonu te tauhaga, kae e kitatou iloa na tutupu i te va o ienei tauhaga e lua.

Ite tauhaga 1986, nae iei te tino Akelohi mai Niu Hila e igoa kia Simon Best na fai ana hukehukega i Tokelau. E lahi lele tona taimi na fai ai ana hukehukega i Fakaofo ma Atafu, kae e heki lahi ni ana galuega na fai i Nukunonu.

Na fakaaoga e Simon Best na metotia iei na takua muamua i Fakaofo. Na hukehuke e ia na koga tau lata atu kite Faleha o te lotu Katoliko. Na lahi lele na mea na maua i lalo o te laukelekele na kitea ai te itukaiga olaga nae ola ai na tino Fakaofo i na aho kua leva. Ko te vaega pe ko te koga maualalo i te laukelekele na maua ai e ia na meakai a na tino, ko ni poga ivi o he fonu. Na fakaaoga la e ia na pogaivi o te fonu ke hakili ai te tauhaga nae ola ai te fonu.

photo: David Addison

photo: Timothy Gallaher

The result showed the turtle lived about 800-500 years ago. Because this bone came from the lowest cultural layer in the excavation, we know that people were living on Fakaofo at least 800-500 years ago. But we don't know if these were the first people or if there are earlier cultural deposits waiting to be discovered someplace else on Fakaofo.

Simon Best also excavated near the back of the Fale Fono on Fakaofo. When he got to the very bottom of the excavation he found hard coral (about 3 metres below the current ground surface). He thought that this coral was the ancient reef of Fakaofo from the time of the Mid-Holocene Highstand when the ocean was 1-2 metres higher. At this time there would have been only a reef at Fakaofo and no dry land. Simon decided to take a piece of the coral and radiocarbon date it.

The date (NZ7449) when the coral was growing was sometime between 2200 years ago and 1800 years ago. This 400 year period is not very precise, but it does give us an idea about when Fakaofo was covered in ocean water.

From the same excavation near the Fale Fono, Simon found a cone shell (NZ7396). He found it at the very bottom of the cultural layers and at the top of the natural beach layers. He thought that this shell might give a better date for when people first arrived on Fakaofo. The shell dates to between 1300 and 1000 years ago. This may mean that there was a beach starting to form at Fale on Fakaofo at that time. Or the shell may be older than the beach and was thrown up there by waves.

Na maua mai i ko te fonu tenei nae ola mai te 800 kite 500 tauhaga kua teka. Ona kote pogaivi tenei na maua mai i te koga pito hili ona maualalao i te hukehukega, e kitaou iloa ai, nae iei na tino nae nonofo i Fakaofo mai te 800 kite 500 tauhaga kua teka. Kae e he mautinoa e ki tatou pe ko ienei na tino muamua na nofoia e kilatou te fenua. Ona e he kitatou iloa pe iei ni ietahi koga kelekele e maua ai ni vaega e i tua atu, kako heki iei ni hukehukega e fai ai.

Na fai foki na hukehukega a Simon Best i tua atu ote Fale Fono o Fakaofo. I te taimi na pa ai ki lalo, pe maua he tolu mita, na tau ki he koga akau/papa maeketu. Na veake ia Simon kote koga papa muamua lava tenei o Fakaofo, mai te taimi nae maualuga ai te tai, ihe tahi kite lua mita. E venei ite taimi tena ko Fakaofo nae he koga papa, kako heki iei ai ni kelekele matutu. Na kave la e Simon he vaega o te papa ke hakili ona tauhaga.

Na maua mai kote lauakau pe ko te koga papa tenei na kamata ola ake ite 2200 kite 1800 tauhaga kua teka. Ona e katoa te 400 tauhaga ite va o na aho ienei e faigata ke iloa tonu he tauhaga, kae e kitaou iloa mai ai, na tauhaga nae i lalo ai ote tai te fenua o Fakaofo.

Mai na galuega lava na fakatino i te tafa fale fono, na maua ai e Simon ni figota, i tana lipotii, kote figota tenei ko he "kalea", kae e he mautinoa pe hako te igoa. Na talitonu ia Simon e manaia te fakaaoga o te figota tenei ke maua ai he tauhaga, e iloa ai pe ko anafea te na omai ai na tino muamua ki Fakaofo. Ko tenei figota na maua ai na tauhaga mai te 1300 kite 1000 tauhaga kua teka. Tona uiga la, na iei te matafaga fou kua kamata oi hula ite tafa ote fale fono ite taimi tenei. Pe kote figota tenei, he mea kua leva atu, kana togi ake ki gauta e te tai.

Atonu e faigata malie oi fuafua na tauhaga na maua mai i na hukehukega a Simon Best na fai i Fakaofo, kako te mea kua kitatou kitea atu, ko he tala faka holopito agai kite tutupu ake o te fenua. Muamua e kitatou kitea na papa pe kote lau akau nae i lalo ote tai, oi hohoko ake ai te matafaga, e heki mataloa atu kae nofoia loa e

Despite the problems in interpreting the dates that Simon Best got from Fakaofo, we can start to see a picture of the history of the island. At first there was a reef covered in water, then later a beach formed, and sometime after that, people arrived and were living on the island. More excavation and more dating samples will help us to better understand the exact timing of these processes.

Simon Best only spent a few days on Nukunonu and did one small excavation. There have never been any radiocarbon dates for Nukunonu. Clearly, it will be important to start archaeological research on Nukunonu so that its ancient history can be better understood. No history of Tokelau would be complete without important information from Tuloto.

On Atafu, Simon Best found one date. It came from an excavation across the road from Filo and Tilaima Filo's house and Patuki and Maine Isaako's house. The sample was charcoal and it came from the lowest cultural layer,

tagata.

E manakomia ke toe fai ni tahi hukehukega kae ke faka mautinoa e kitatou te taimi tonu na tutupu ai na vaega kehekehe ienei.

E heki lahi ni aho mo Simon Best i Nukunonu, ko teia na fokotahi ai lava te koga na hukehuke e ia. E heki iei foki ni vaega na fakaaoga e Simon ke maua mai ai ni tauhaga mo Nukunonu. Atonu ko tenei e manakomia lahi ai, te fai o ni hukehukega i Nukunonu kae ke malamalama atili ai kitatou ki na aho kua leva. E he mafai ke katotoa ni tala agai ki Tokelau, kafai e he maua mai ni a tatou tala faka holopito mai te Tuloto.

E fokotahi he vaega na fakaaoga e Simon Best ke maua mai ai he tauhaga mai i Atafu. Na maua mai i he koga e fakafegai ma te fale o Filo ma Tilaima Filo ma te fale o Patuki ma Maine Isaako. Ko te vaega na fakaaoga ko ni malala, na maua mai i te koga laukelekele e talitonu na nofoia ai na tino muamua o Atafu. Na maua na tauhaga o te malala, mai te 1200 kite 700 tauhaga kua teka. Atonu ko ienei tauhaga na maua mai e he hako. Ka ko

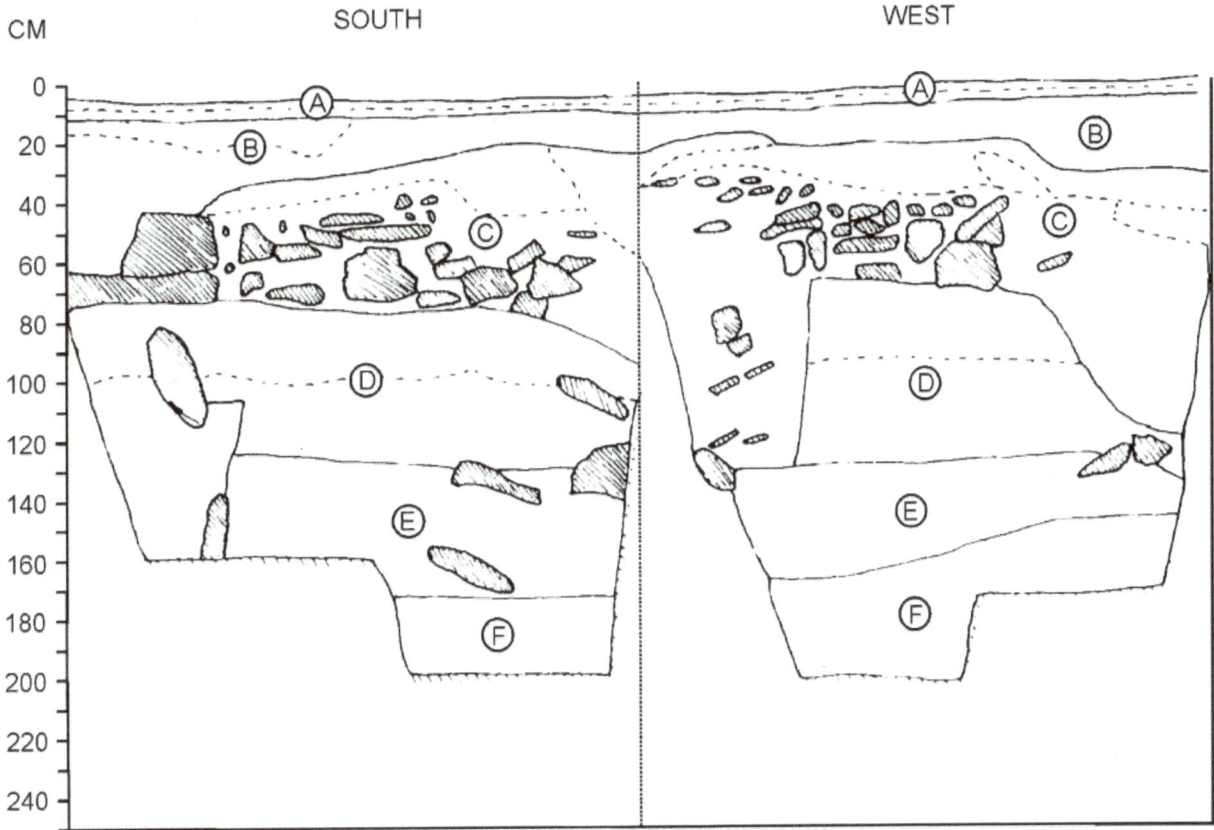

Above: Simon Best TP4 profile drawing. Courtesy of Simon Best and Andrew McAlister.

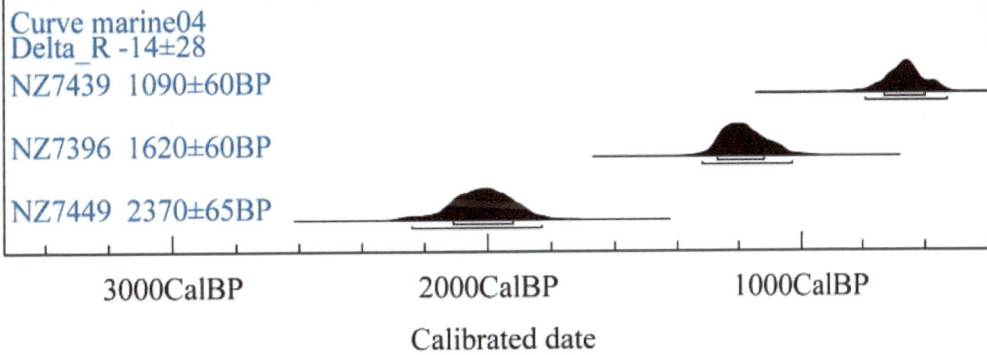

Marine data from Hughen et al (2004);Delta_R -14±28;OxCal v3.10 Bronk Ramsey (2005): cub r:5 sd:12 prob usp[chron]

Curve marine04
Delta_R -14±28
NZ7439 1090±60BP
NZ7396 1620±60BP
NZ7449 2370±65BP

3000CalBP   2000CalBP   1000CalBP

Calibrated date

Above: Three dates from Simon Best's excavations on Fakaofo

photo: David Addison

just above an ancient natural beach. The date is sometime between 1200 and 700 years ago. Unfortunately, this is a very imprecise date. The only thing we can say is that we know that people were already living on Atafu at sometime during this period. But we don't know exactly when it was.

So, much remains to be done to understand the human history of Tokelau. So far, we can say that people were living on at least two atolls sometime in the general period of 1200 to 500 years ago. Much more archaeological excavation and dating from every nuku of Tokelau will be needed before we can have a clearer understanding of when people first arrived and where they first settled.

te mea e mautinoa e kitatou, nae iei ni tino nae i luga o te fenua i te piliota tenei. Kae e he mautinoa tonu na tauhaga nae kinei ai.

E lahi lele na galuega koi tatau ke fai, ke malamalama atili ai kitatou ki na tala faka holopito o tagata Tokelau. E venei ite taimi nei, e mafai kitatou ke lea, nae lua ia motu o Tokelau nae nofoia mai te 1200 kite 500 tauhaga kua teka. Kae e manakomia ke fai ni hukehukega faka Akelohi, mai na motu uma o Tokelau ke malamalama atili kitatou pe ko fea te na omamai ai na tino Tokelau, ma na koga o na motu na nofoia e kilatou.

WHERE DID THE FIRST TOKELAUANS COME FROM?

This question can be answered using a variety of scientific techniques. These include: artefact shapes; artefact geochemistry; human DNA; and animal DNA.

NA OMAMAI I FEA NA TINO MUAMUA O TOKELAU?

E lahi lele ni metotia faka haienihi e mafai ke tali ai tenei fehili. Fakatakitakiga, e mafai ke fakaaoga e kitatou na vaega e maua mai i luga pe ko lalo o te lauklekele, fakatahi ai ma na vaega e takua ko ni DNA mai na tagata ma na meaola. Manatua kona DNA ko ni mea e fau ai o tatou tino, e kehekehe uma na DNA o na tino tautokatahi, veia ma na meaola.

photo: David Addison

ARTEFACT SHAPES

Archaeologists use the "artefact" to mean the things that people make and use. In traditional times in Tokelau everything that people used was made by them or was brought from other islands. Many of these things do not last in the soil. So archaeologists almost never find things like mats and bowls and other things made from plants (unless they were burned and turned into charcoal). But archaeologists do find things made from rock and shell and bone. Simon Best found thinks like fishhooks and ornaments made out of shell and bone.

People usually make things that look similar to the things that their parents made. Sometimes people change the design or shape of things they make. Over many generations this can lead to artefacts that look different.

What this means is that the first people in Tokelau probably made things that looked very similar to the original island they came from. What we need to do is to find the earliest settlements in Tokelau and date them. We can then compare the artefacts from those earliest settlements to artefacts from outside islands from the same date. This will give us a good idea of where the first Tokelau people came from.

It is important to do this on each atoll in Tokelau. That will allow us to understand if all of Tokelau was settled from the same place, of if perhaps different atolls were settled by people from different origin islands.

ARTEFACT GEOCHEMISTRY

Artefacts have more information than just their shapes. Especially artefacts made from stone. Of course the only stone from Tokelau is coral rock. But Simon Best found tools made from volcanic rock. This rock had to come from a high volcanic island such as Samoa, Uvea, Tonga, or Rarotonga.

Each volcano has a slightly different mix of minerals and elements in it. This is the rock's "geochemistry". Because of each island's different geochemistry, it is possible to know what island volcanic rocks come from.

Simon Best found stone tools from Fakaofo, Nukunonu and Atafu that were made from a kind of rock called "basalt". The geochemistry of these tools shows that they all came from Tutuila. In addition, the Atafu and Nukunonu tools appear to have come from a specific quarry on Tutuila called Tataga Matau in Leone Village.

TE TINO O NA MEA E MAUA MAI I LUGA PE KO LALO O TE LAUKELEKELE.

I te matakupu tenei ko te Akelohi, ko na mea e maua i luga pe ko lalo ote laukelekele, ni mea na fau pe na fakaaoga e tagata. I na aho kua leva, ko na mea uma nae fakaaoga e tagata o Tokelau, ko ni mea na fau lava e kilatou, pe na kaumai mai na tahi fenua. Ko te lahiga o na mea ienei, e he mataloa lele i lalo o te kelekele kae pala.Ko te mafuaga ia, e he lahi maua ai e na tino Akelohi ni mea e fau mai na lakau. Fakatakitakiga, e ve ko ni moega, ipukai e fau mai te lakau, vagana la ko na mea ienei na huhunu kae liu malala. Ko te lahiga o na mea e maua ko na mea e fau mai i na fatu, figota, pe ko na pogaivi. Na maua e Simon Best ni vaega venei e fau mai i na figota ma na pogaivi.

Ko tagata e lahi fau lava e kilatou ni mea e ve lava kona kope na fai e o latou matua. I na tahi taimi e mafai ke hui te faiga o na mea e fau e tagata, fakatakitakiga e mafai ke hui te tino o te kope teia e fai. Kafai la e tutupu tenei vaega mai teia augatupulaga ki te tahi augatupulaga, e lahi lele he huiga ki te kope tenei. Tona uiga e lahi lele he kehekehega o te tino ote kope na kamata mai ai, kite mea kua iei ai.

Ko tona uiga, e tatau ke tai tutuha na kope a na tino muamua o Tokelau, ki na kope a na fenua na omamai ai. Ko te mea e tatau ke fai, ko te hakili na koga ma ni vaega mai na tino na nofoia muamua e kilatou na fenua, oi hakili loa pe ko tea te tauhaga nae iei ai. E mafai ai ke fakatuhahua na tauhaga ona kope iena, kina kope e maua mai i na tahi fenua mai te vaitimi tena. Atonu e maua ai he tali agai ki te fehili, pe ko fea te na omamai ai ia tagata Tokelau.

E taua ke fai tenei galuega ina motu uma o Tokelau. E kitatou iloa ai, pe ko na motu o Tokelau na nofoia, e ni tino e omamai i he fenua e fokotahi, pe ni tino na omamai i ni fenua kehekehe.

NA KOPE E FAI I NA FATU

E he gata ona maua ni tala e kitaou mai te tino ma na foliga o na kope e maua i lalo ma luga o te laukelekele, kae lahi foki ni tala e mafai ke maua mai i na kope e fai i na fatu. E fokotahi lava te itukaiga fatu e maua i Tokelau, ko na fatu papa/lau akau. Kae i na hukehukega a Simon Best, na maua ai e ia ni fatu e fau mai i na mauga mu. Atonu, ko te fatu tenei na tatau ke hau mai i na fenua iei e fau mai i na mauga mu, e ve ko Samoa,Uvea, Tonga pe ko Rarotonga.

Ko na mauga mu e kehekehe uma ina vaega e fau ai. Ona la e kehekehe uma na fenua iei e fau mai i na mauga mu, e mafai ke iloa e kitatou pe ko fea te fenua e hau ai he itukaiga fatu. Na iei na kope e veia ko na toki nae fau mai i ni fatu mai ni mauga mu,na

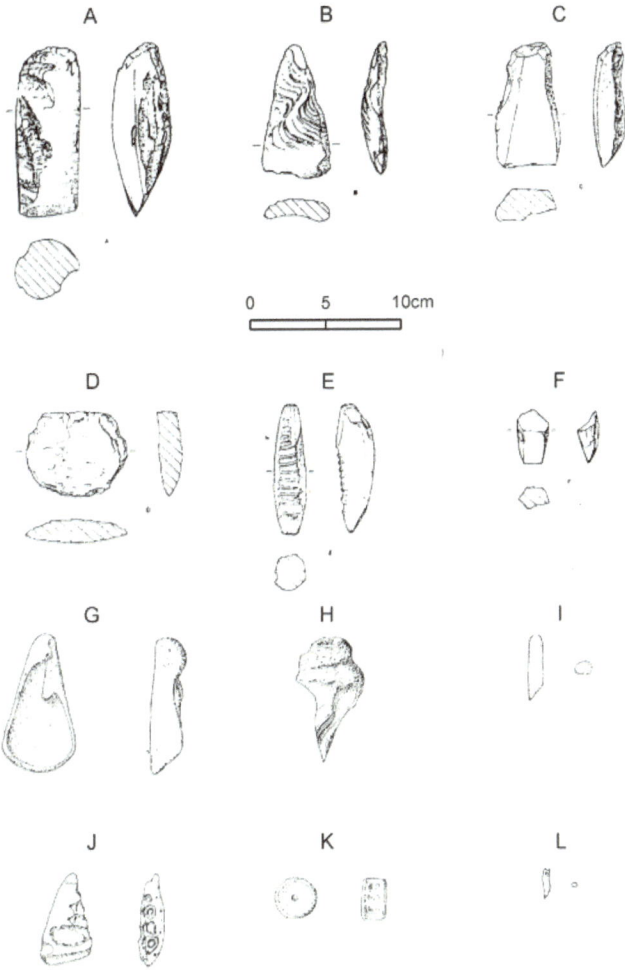

Left and Below: Artifacts excavated by Simon best. Courtesy of Simon Best and Andrew McAlister.

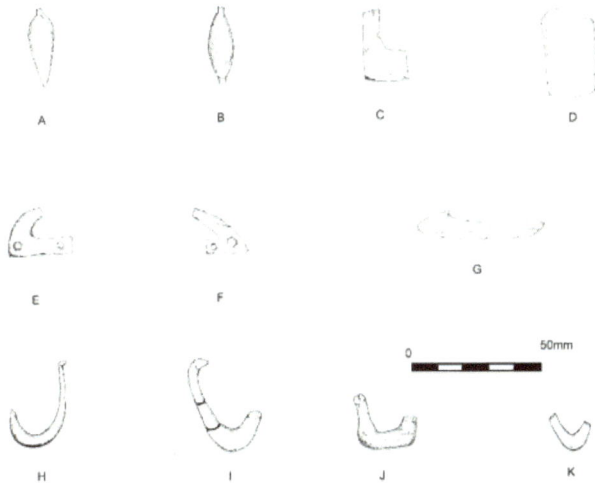

Above: Examples of basalt stone tools from Tutuila. Collected on Tutuila.

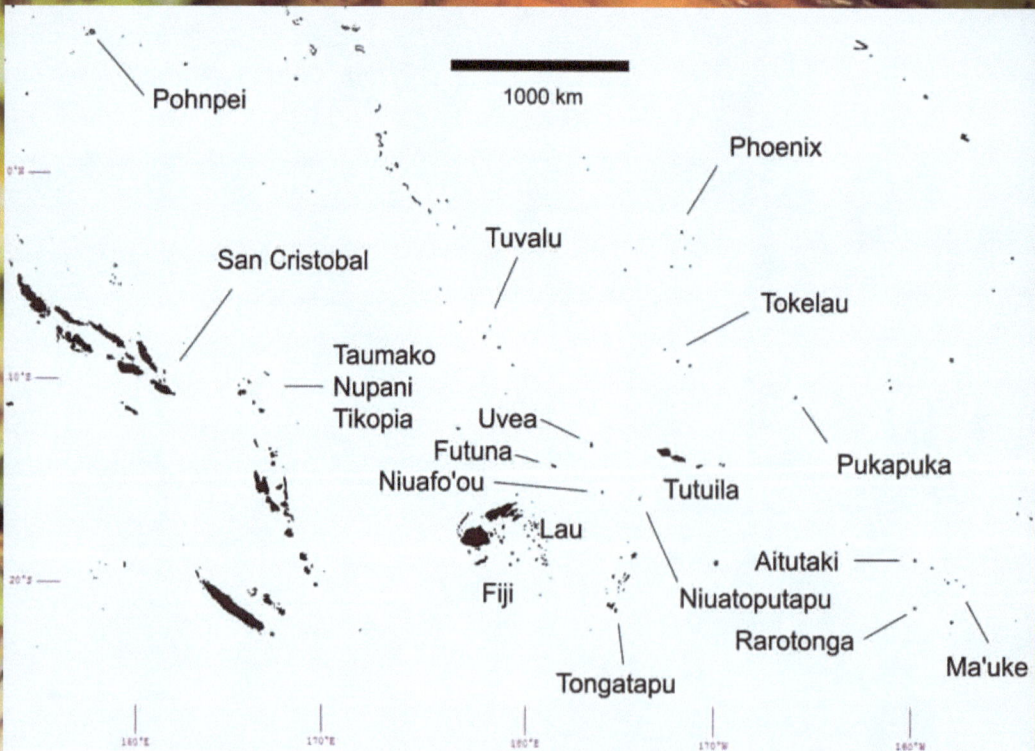

Above: map showing islands where Tutuila basalt tools have been found by archaeologists. Base map courtesy of Peter Minton (http://www.evs-islands.blogspot.com).

Interestingly, there is an oral tradition from Leone that tells of two brothers from Tokelau called Punaloa and Punamai.

We don't know if Simon Best's stone artefacts are from the earliest settlers of Tokelau. But this gives us an indication of how powerful stone geochemistry is for tracing connections between islands. What we can say for now is that there was contact between Tutuila and Tokelau in ancient times. Much more work needs to be done to find stone artefacts from the earliest settlers of Tokelau to help trace where they came from.

HUMAN DNA

Every human has a genetic code in every cell of their body. This genetic code is called DNA. This is what tells our body how to form, what colour hair to make, what shape to make our nose, what colour to make our eyes. We inherit half of our DNA from our mother and half from our father. And every individual's DNA is unique to them.

By tracing the paths of DNA back in time, we can see who is related. For example, everyone with the same grandmother will have some of her DNA. And the same is true back to great-great-great grandmothers and even farther back in time.

maua e Simon Best i Fakaofo, Nukunonu ma Atafu. Na hukehuke na fatu ienei, kae maua mai ko ni fatu na kaumai i Tutuila. Ko na fatu foki mai Nukunonu ma Atafu nae tutuha tona fauhaga pe ko na vaega na fau ai, ma na fatu i te koga o Tutuila e igoa kia Tataga Matau i te nuku o Leone. E iei foki na tala tuku mai te nuku tenei o Leone, e fakamatala ai ni uho e igoa kia Punaloa ma Punamai mai Tokelau.

E he kitaou mautinoa pe ko na kope na maua e Simon Best, pe ni kope mai na tino muamua na nofoia e kilatou ia Tokelau. Kae e kitatou loa te manaia o na metotia e mafai ke fakaaoga i na fatu e maua, ke hakili ai na hokotaga o Tokelau ma ie tahi fenua.Mo te taimi nei, e kitatou iloa nae iei na hokotaga o Tokelau ma Tutuila i na aho kua leva. E tatau ke fai ni galuega ke maua mai ai ni kope e fau i te fatu, kae ke mafai ke hakili pe ko fea tena omamai ai ia tiagata Tokelau.

NA VAEGA E FAU AI TE TAGATA

I ho he tagata, e iei na vaega e takua ko ni DNA. Ko na mea ienei te ia fakatonutonua pe vefea ona fau o tatou tino. Fakataki-takiga, e ia faia o tatou foliga, e ve ko te lanu o to ulu, pe he itukaiga ihu vefea to koe, pe vefea te lanu o mata. Ko te DNA ote tino e maua mai i ona matua,ko te tahiafa e maua mai ite tamana, ma te tahi afa e maua mai ite matua.E kehekehe uma na DNA o na tino tautokatahi.

Kafai kitatou e hukehuke kina DNA i na aho kua leva, e mafai ke kitatou iloa pe ko ai na tino e kaiga. Fakatakitakiga, uma na tino

David Addison

There are two ways to examine DNA. The first is by looking at the DNA of living people. For example, by comparing the DNA of everyone on an island with people from other islands, we can see who shares ancestors. When we find connections, this means that people's marriage partners were coming from outside islands.

This is a powerful technique, because it is relatively easy to get DNA from living people (a simple wipe from inside the mouth) and a whole population can be sampled to find out all of the possible connections with outside islands.

The problem with this kind of analysis is that we don't know when the outside DNA arrived on the island. Was it 2 generations ago? Or 8? Or was it from the first settlers of Tokelau?

To solve this problem archaeologists can take samples from ancient bones. It is very hard to get DNA from ancient bones, but team member Professor Lisa Matisoo-Smith is an expert in this.

Of course, any sampling of modern or ancient DNA depends on permission from the nuku. So these kinds of information can only be obtained if the nuku decides that it wants this done.

Lisa Matisoo-Smith

e tutuha o latou tupuna, e maua uma e kilatou he vaega o te DNA o to latou tupuna. E hei he kehekehega, ke pa lava ki he fia tupulaga kua teka, e mafai lava ke hakili to hokotaga kina tupulaga kua teka, e auala mai i na DNA.

E lua ia auala e mafai ke hukehuke ai na DNA, ko te vaega muamua e mafai ke kikila kina DNA o na tino koi ola. Fakatakitakiga e mafai ke fakatuhatuha e kitatou na DNA o na tino i he fenua, ma ni tahi tino o he tahi fenua. Kafai e kitatou kitea e iei ni hokotaga, e kitatou iloa, e iei ni tino na fai kaiga kini tino mai te tahi fenua.

E manaia tenei metotia ona e faigofie ona maua mai na DNA mai na tino ola, e mafai ke maua mai i na faua e hoholo mai i loto o to gutu.Ko te fakafitauli i tenei galuega, e he kitatou iloa pe ko anafea tena maua ai na DNA fou. Pe kua lua pe valu ia tupulaga kua teka atu? Pe na maua mai i na tino na nofoia muamua e kilatou ia Tokelau?

Ke fofo tenei fakafitauli, e hukehuke e na tino Akelohi na pogaivi ona tino i na aho kua leva. E faigata malie tenei galuega, kae e mafai ke fai e te tahi Haienitihi i tenei polokalame, ko te matua kia Professor Lisa Martisoo Smith.

E maina lele, ko ho he galuega e fai ki he pogaivi e maua i te taimi o na hukehukega, e muamua ona foki mai te fakatagaga mai te nuku. Tona uiga, mo ni tala ke maua mai i na itukaiga hukehukega venei, e maua lava te tonu mai te nuku.

photo: Rintaro Ono

photo: Timothy Gallaher

ANIMAL DNA

Just like humans, animals have DNA as well. The same kinds of analyses can be done on animals like rats, pigs, chickens, and even dogs.

People brought these animals to Tokelau. So the DNA of the animals can be compared to the DNA of animals on outside islands and we can start to see where there are connections.

The same ideas apply to animals as to humans. Looking at the living individuals gives us a big sample, but its hard to know when the contacts with outside happened. Again, archaeological samples from the earliest settlements can be used to find out the origin of the first Tokelau settlers.

RESOURCE MANAGEMENT

Tokelau's natural resources can be divided into two categories: marine resources and land (or terrestrial) resources. Each of these categories can be investigated using different scientific techniques.

NA VAEGA E FAU AI NA MEAOLA

E ve lava ko te tagata, ko na meaola foki e iei o latou DNA. E mafai foki lava ke fai ni hukehukega kina meaola e ve ko te kimoa, pua, moa ma na maile. Ko na meaola na kaumai e na tino ki Tokelau. E mafai foki ke fakatuhatuha na DNA o na meaola mai Tokelau kina DNA o na meaola mai na nuku i fafo, ke kitea ai foki e kitatou na hokotaga.

E tutuha la te agaga e fia fai ai na galuega ki na DNA o tagata fakatahi ai ma na meaola. Ko te hukehuke kina DNA o na tino e ola e maua ai na tala, kako te fakafitauili e he mautino pe na kamata afea na hokotaga. Kafai la e maua ni vaega e mafai ke hukehuke mai na aho kua leva, e ve ko ni pogaivi, e mafai ke kitatou iloa pe ko fea tena omamai ai na tino muamua o Tokelau.

PULEPULEGA ONA LIHOHI

E mafai ke vaevae e kitatou na lihohi faka te natula o Tokelau kini vaega e lua. Te vaega muamua ko na lihohi i te tai, ma te tahi vaega, ko na lihohi i te laukelekele. E lahi na itukaiga metotia faka haienihi ke fakaaoga ke hukehuke ai na vaega ienei.

Ona kote he lahi o na lihohi i luga o Tokelau, nae iei na

Because of the very limited range of natural resources on the atolls, Tokelau's people have had to develop very sophisticated resource management strategies. This insured that over the centuries sustainably used resources were passed on to each succeeding generation.

MARINE RESOURCES

Archaeologists can study ancient marine resource use by looking at the remains of the food people caught in the past. Most people can easily see how shells can be identified. When you see certain shells in a layer, you know people were eating that food. Giant clam (faihua) is a good example.

Alex Morrison

Team member Alex Morrison from the University of Hawai'i will be studying ancient patterns of shellfish use in Tokelau. He has previously done this kind of study in Samoa, Fiji, and Hawai'i.

Dr. Rintaro Ono can identify fish from their bones. By looking at all of the fish bones from an excavation and identifying the different quantities of each kind of fish, Dr. Ono can help us understand how ancient people managed their fish resources.

auala ma na metotia na fakaaoga e tagata Tokelau ke fuafua lelei ai ana lihohi. Na mautinoa ai ko te fakahoahoa lelei o ana lihohi e mafai ke fakaauau ai na lihohi mo ietahi augatupulaga.

NA LIHOHI ITE TAI

E mafai ke hukehuke e na tino Akelohi na lihohi ite tai i na aho kua leva, kafai e hukehuke agai kina meakai a na tino nae maua i na aho kua leva. E kitea gofie foki e na tino na itukaiga meakai nae kai e na tino i na aho kua leva. Fakatakitakiga, kafai e tau atu ki he koga ote laukelekele e tumu i na atigi fahua, e keiloa kona tino nae kai fahu ite taimi tena.

Ko te tahi tino ote tenei polokalame ia Alex Morrison mai te Iunivehite o Hawai'i, e fakamoemoe e fai ana hukehukega kite fakaaogaga o na figota o te tai i na aho kua leva e tagata o Tokelau. Nae fai muamua e ia na itukaiga hukehukega venei i Samoa, Fiti ma Hawai'i.

Ko Dr. Rintaro Ono e ia iloa na itukaiga ika mai ona pogaivi. E mafai ke kitatou iloa pe na vefea ona pulepule vefea e tagata Tokelau ana ika, kafai e kikila ia Dr.Ono kina itukaiga ika e maua ma te fuainumela o na ika e maua i lalo o te laukelekele.

photo: Rintaro Ono

A previous study was done on fish bones that Simon Best excavated on Fakaofo. Andrew McAlister's study is available as a downloadable PDF file at our project website: www.tokelauscience.com

TERRESTRIAL RESOURCES

Atoll islands like those of Tokelau are very unique and special ecosystems completely unlike high volcanic islands or continents. The land is built upon the remains of coral and the soil is formed from sand and whatever organic matter is able to accumulate. Within the ground, a thin water lens supports the plant whose roots help to hold the sand in place.

Atolls are also the landforms most strongly influenced by the sea. Ocean currents, waves, and storm surge daily shape the atoll islets, sometimes building new land and at other times eroding the land away. Atolls are also strongly affected by weather, with drought and tropical storms being important factors that influence life on atolls. Due

Rintaro Ono

Nae iei fok ni galuega venei na fai muamua i na pogaivi ona ika na maua mai ina galuega a Simon Best na fai i Fakaofo. Ko na galuega ienei na fai e Andrew McAliister, e mafai ke faitau ma malamalama atili ko ki ei, kafai koe e fano ki te mea e maua uma ai na vaega o te polokame tenei ite initaneti: www.tokelauscience.com.

LIHOHI O TE LAUKELEKELE

E lahi lele te kehekehega o na itukaiga hikomaga e iei ai na fenua e fau mai ite lau akau ve ko Tokelau, mai na fenua e fau mai i na mauga mu. Ko te fenua e fau i luga ote lau akau, ko te laukelekele e fau mai i te oneone ma ie tahi mea i te hikomaga e ake. I lalo ote laukeleke ko te vai e e fehoahoani ke taofia e ia na lakau, kako te aka ote lakau e taofia e ia te oneone. Ko na fenua venei foki, e lahi ona fai kiei ni huiga mai te tai. Ko te tai, ma na galu ma ni matagi malolohi e hui lava e ia te tino ote fenua i aho takitahi. I na tahi taimi e fau e ia ni fenua fou, i na tahi taimi kua kai, pe tokehea foki e ia ni koga fenua. Ko na fenua venei, lahi foki hona afainaga mai te tau, kae maihe na mugala, ma na matamatagi malolohi pe ko na afa. Ona foki la ko na vaega ienei, e faigata ai ona lahi ni meaola ma ni lakau

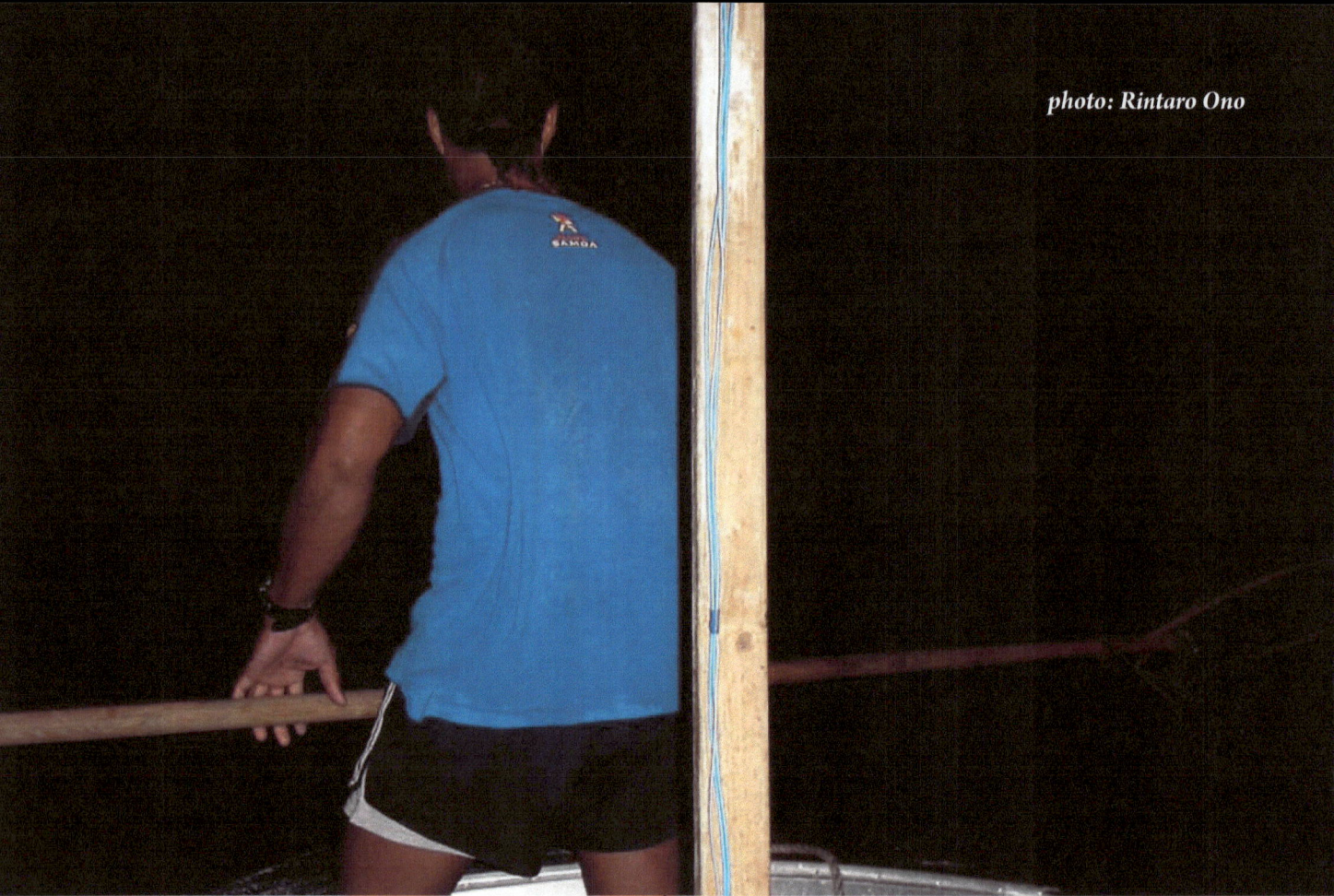

to the combined effect of these forces, very few plants and animals are able to survive on atolls.

The atoll ecosystem would appear to provide very few terrestrial resources for humans to survive. However, the people of Tokelau have thrived by developing innovative ways to use, manage, and share their resources, insuring that the resources are plentiful enough to support their population without using so much as to jeopardize the environment or reduce the supply for future generations.

The traditional resource management practices of Tokelau can serve as a sustainable model for the world. Such models are increasingly important as more people realize that they have overexploited their resources and damaged the ability of their environment to support their own populations.

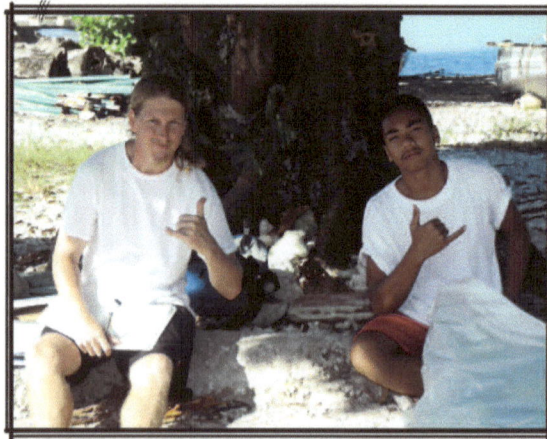

e ola i na itukaiga fenua venei ko Tokelau.

Ko te itukaiga hikomaga tenei, e he lai ni ana lihohi i luga o te laukelekele. Kako tagata Tokelau, e ola pea ona na iei na auala ma na metotia na fakaaoga, ma pulepule ma fakahoahoa ai ana lihohi, ma mautinoa e lava ana lihohi ke fafaga ma ola ai ona tagata kae he afaina ai te hikohikomaga, ma lava na lihohi mo na tupulaga i te lumanaki.

Ko te itukaiga pulepulega kina lihohi ienei na fakaaoga e Tokelau, e mafai ke kavea ma takiala mo te lalolagi. E taua lele ienei itukaiga metotia, ona kua fatoa kitea e na tahi tino te hona fakaaoga o a latou lihohi, ma kua afaina atu ai te hikohikomaga, ke pa kite tulaga teia kua he lava te fakahoa mo ona tagata.

Ko te vaega tenei e hukehuke kiei te tahi tino o tenei polokalame e igoa kia Timothy Gallaher mai te Iunivehite o Hawai'i. E lahi lele te taimi e talatalanoa ai ia Tim ma na tino o na motu takitahi, ma fai e ia ni fakamaumauga agai kite fakahoahoaga ona lihohi o te laukelekele, veia ko na ulu, na fala, na pulaka, na niu ma ietahi mea.

Timothy Gallaher from the University of Hawai'i will study this topic. By having detailed talks with people in each nuku, Tim will document how each nuku uses and manages its terrestrial resources such as breadfruit (ulu), pandanus (fala), pulaka, coconuts, etc.

Tim's work in Tokelau focuses on recording and preserving traditional resource management practices. In order to do this he must assess what natural resources are being used today and what resources were once used by past generations of Tokelauans.

We need to understand what practices are or were in place to prevent overexploitation of those resource or damage to the habitat that supports those resources. Sometimes these management practices are well known and clearly serve to protect a resource. At other times a management practice is found in the form of a cultural activity which may not appear to be directly related to resource conservation but which in fact serves to ensure that a resource is not overly harvested. Finally, the man-

Ko te galuega a Tim e fai i Tokelau, kote fakamaumauga o na auala nae fakaaoga e tagata o Tokelau, kite pulepulega o ana lihohi. Ke mafai ke fakatino tenei vaega, he tatau ke kikila agai kina lihohi e fakaaoga i na aho nei, ma na lihohi nae fakaaoga e na tupulaga o Tokelau kua teka atu.

E tatau ke manino na fakatinoga e fai pe nae fai, nae faka mautinoa ai te he hona fakaaoga o na lihohi, pe afaina te hiko-maga e iei ai na lihohi. Ko na tahi taimi ko na pulepulega ienei e iloa ma matea ai, na fai ke puipui ai he lihohi. I na tahi taimi ko he itukaiga pulepulega e fakatino, mo te he hona fakaaoga o he lihohi. Ma te tahi mea, e venei ko na pulepulega ienei nae fakatino kua he manatua, kae e venei e manatua ini tala tuku pe ni tala kakai, i ni pehe, pe manatua foki e ni tino matutua.

Ke malamalama atili kitatou kite hikohikomaga i luga ote laukelekele, e tatau ke manino muamua kitatou pe ko nia na lakau e ola ite taimi nei i luga o na motu. Te tahi tino hukehuke kina lakau kua lauiloa foki ana galuega i te Pahefika, ko tona igoa ko Dr. Art Whistler, e fakamaumau uma e ia na lakau e maua i Fakaofo, Nukunonu ma Atafu. E taua lele ke lihi uma na lakau,

photo: Timothy Gallaher

photo: *Timothy Gallaher*

agement activity may no longer be practiced but may be remembered in the form of legends, songs, or in the memories of the elders.

To understand the current terrestrial environment of Tokelau, it is important to have a precise understanding of what plants are currently growing on each island. Dr. Art Whistler, one of the most knowledgeable and experienced Pacific botanists will make a complete list of all of the plant species growing on Fakaofo, Nukunonu, and Atafu. This will also help to understand changes in the future. It is impossible to know if change has occurred if we do not have an accurate record of what exists now.

Understanding the ancient past of terrestrial resource use is much more difficult. Remains of plants usually rot quickly in Tokelau's wet and hot climate. So, we must search for the clues that have survived from ancient times.

ka eke kitaou iloa ni huiga i te lumanaki, aua e he mafai ke kitatou iloa pe iei ni huiga, vagana kua tuhituhi ma fakamaumau fakalelei.

E faigata malie ke kitatou iloa te fakaaogaga o na lihohi o te laukelekele i na aho kua leva. Ona ko te tau o Tokelau e lahi huhu ma vevela, kona lakau e pala gofie i te kelekele. Ko teia e tatau ai ke hukehuke agai kini mea na ola mai ina aho kua leva.

Ko na malala, ko ni mea e he vave pala, e mafai ke fano te fia afe o tauhaga ei lalo ai ote laukelekele. Kafai la e iei ni lakau na huhunu, e liu malala ma he toe mafai ke pala i lalo o te kelekele. E iei la na metotia faka haienihi e mafai ke kikila ai kina malala, ma iloa pe ni itukaiga lakau a iena. E iei na tahi tino ote polokalame tenei e igoa kia Jeff Boutain mai te Iunivehite o Hawai'i, ma Jen Huebert mai te Iunivehite o Aukilani e hukehuke e kilaua na malala e kaumai i na galuega e fakatino i Tokelau.

Above: Art Whistler

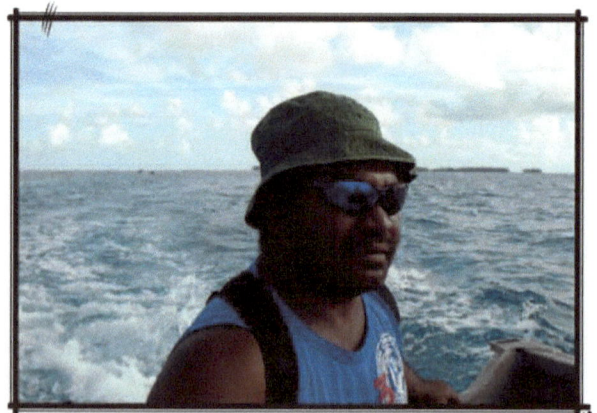

Charcoal is very durable. It will last for thousands of years in the soil and never decay. So, when plant parts are burned they can be preserved almost forever. Even better, many kinds of plants can be identified by microscopically looking at their charcoal. This is because each plant has a slightly different pattern in the way their cells are arranged. Jeff Boutain from the University of Hawai'i and Jen Huebert from the University of Auckland will both work on identifying charcoal from Tokelau excavations.

Land snails are another way to understand the ancient terrestrial environment. These tiny creatures that live under leaves and rocks can be good indicators of the what the environment was like in ancient times. Professor Carl Christensen is a world authority on Pacific land snails. He and Adam Thompson will identify land snails from different excavation layers at each nuku. This will help us understand changes in the Tokelau environment from the time of the first settlers.

E mafai foki ke malamalama kitatou kina lihohi ote laukelekele kafai e hukehuke agai kina meaola ieia e takua kona hihi. Ko na meaola ienei e nonofofo i lalo o na lakau ma na fatu, e mafai ke foki mai e ia he tatou malamalamaga agai kite itukaiga hikomaga nae iei i na aho kua leva. E iei te tahi tino lauiloa i te lalolagi i na hukehukega o na hihi e maua ite Pahefika, ko tona igoa ko Professor Carl Christensen. E galulue fakatahi ma te tahi tino ote polokalame nei ko Adam Thompson, ke kikila agai kina hihi e maua i na motu o Tokelau, kae ke malamalama atili kitatou kina huiga kite hikohikomaga mai lava ite taimi na nofoia muamua ai ia Tokelau.

photo: Hilary Scothorn

photo: Hilary Scothorn

ATAFU AUGUST 2008 FIELDWORK

Our Atafu fieldwork took place 10 August to 8 September 2008. We had to plan for this time because of the Pacific Arts Festival schedule. After spending two happy weeks with the malaga to the Pacific Arts Festival on Tutuila, the off-island project members travelled by sailboat from Pago Pago to Atafu. It took two days to make this trip.

GALUEGA NA FAI I ATAFU ITE 2008

Na fai na galuega i Atafu mai te aho 10 o Aukuho kite aho 8 o Setema 2008. Na fuafua ki te taimi tenei, ona ko te fakatahiga faka te aganuku a te Pahefika teia na fai i Tutuila. Na iei foki te avanoa na mafuta ai ma te kau Malaga a Atafu mo he lua vaiaho i Tutuila,kako heki Malaga atu ki Atafu i na vaka faila.

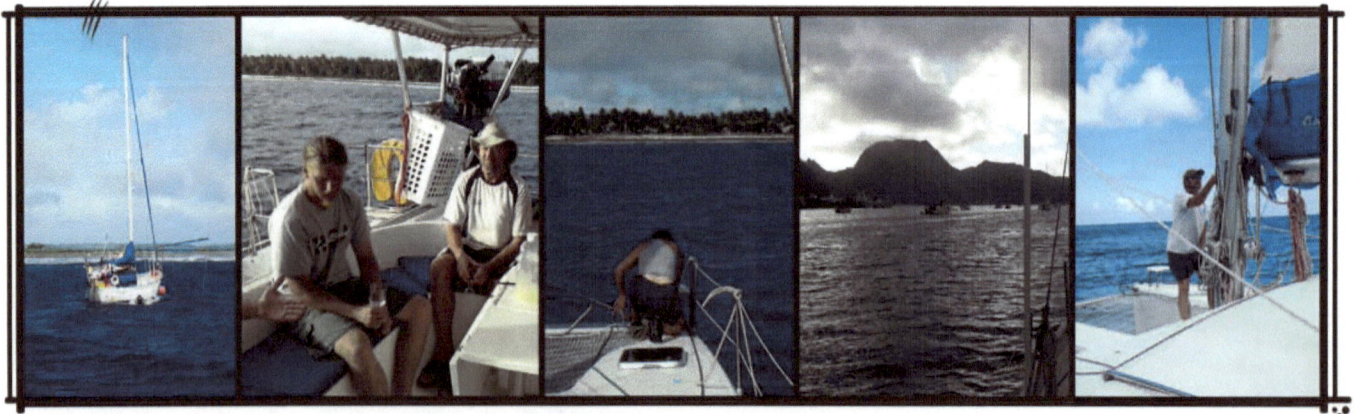

photos: Bryon Bass, Timali Pele, Adam Thompson, David Funk, and Rintaro Ono

Anne and Barry Lange of "Cat's Paw IV" carried American Samoa Community College student Timali Pele and University of Otago student Adam Thompson, an American Samoa Community College student Marie Fa'atuala, Photographer Bryon Bass and researchers Rintaro Ono, Timothy Gallaher, and David Addison sailed on "5th Season" with Gail and David Funk. Our thanks to these two sailing families without whom the off-island team members would have been late for the project. They also stayed on Atafu and helped with the fieldwork.

August is a bad time for the USP students to participate in project because of many commitments to their USP courses. In future years we will schedule fieldwork to coincide with the USP holiday period in June-July.

Na fakaaoga te vaka faila o Anne ma Barry Lange e takua kote "Cat's Paw IV", ke momoli atu ai te kau malaga ki Atafu. Ko te malaga tenei nae iei ai na tamaiti aoga o American Samoa Community College ko Timali Pele ma Marie Fa'atuala, ma he tamaiti aoga mai te Iunivehite o Otago ko Adam Thompson. Na malaga mai ai foki he tino pukeata ko Bryon Bass, ma te tahi tino hukehuke ko Dr. Rintaro Ono. Ko Timothy Gallagher ma Dr. David Addison na malaga ite tahi vaka faila e takua kote "5th Season", e o he ulagali e igoa kia Gail ma David Funk. E momoli foki te fakafetai kina kaiga ienei e lua, aua kana he maua te latou fehoahoani na tuai te kau malaga ki Atafu. Na nonofo foki na kaiga ienei kina galuega na fai i Atafu.

Ko tamaiti aoga ote USP, nae he lahi avanoa ite mahina tenei o Aukuho, ona foki nae lahi feataui kina taimi o na tapenapenaga kina hukega. E iei la na fuafuaga mo te lumanaki ke fakatino na galuega ite taimi kua tukua ai te USP mai te mahina o Iuni kia Iulai.

photo: Hilary Scothorn

photos: Bryon Bass, Timali Pele, Adam Thompson, David Funk, and Rintaro Ono

The first task for the fieldwork was to do an archaeological survey of all of Atafu's land area. This meant walking over the motus and examining all of the ground surface for evidence of past human use. At the same time, Rintaro started his study of fish and Tim started his study on plants. Thanks to the Taupulega for assigning Tene Aluia and Hale Kalolo to help us with our research.

After searching uta for archaeological sites, the archaeologists focussed on excavating on Fale islet. We took

Te galuega muamua na tatau ke fai, kote kikila ki luga o te laukelekele ma fakamaumau na vaega i luga o na koga fenua. Ko tona uiga la, na manakomia ke havavali i luga uma o te laukelekele o Atafu, ke kitea ai ni vaega nae fakaaoga i na aho kua leva. I te taimi nae fakatino ai tenei galuega, kua kamata ai foki na galuega a Dr. Ono ki te hukehukega ona ika, ma Tim kua kamata ana galuega kina lakau. E fakafetai atu foki kite Taupulega o Atafu, mo te faka avanoa o Tene Aluia ma Hale Kalolo, ke fehoahoani kite polokalame.

photo: Timali Pele

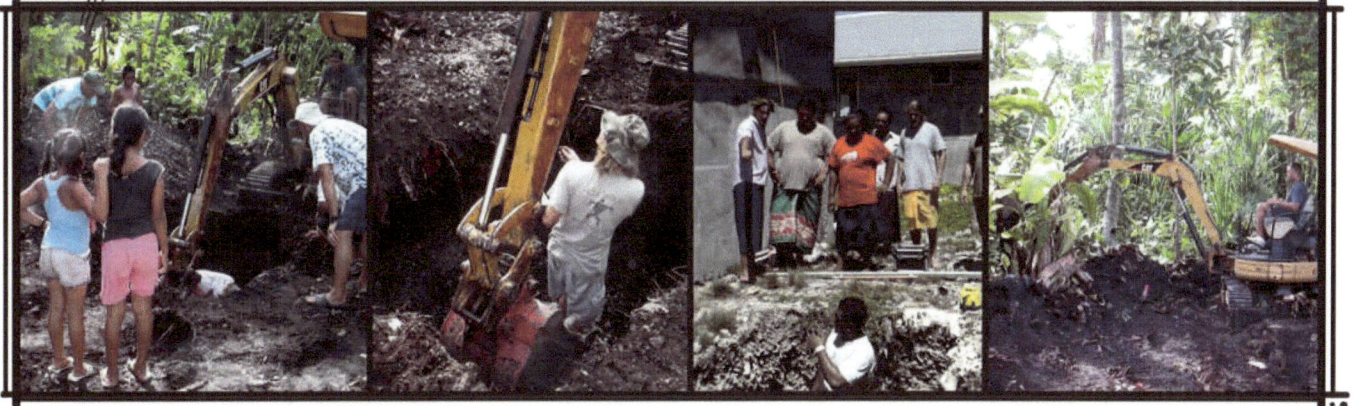

photos: David Funk and Rintaro Ono

advantage of places where Tony was already digging holes for septic tanks. This allowed us to see the stratigraphy before we started and so we could focus on places where we knew there was a good record of cultural deposits.

We were fortunate to be in Atafu for the and Aho o te Mafutaga a Tina and Aho o te Aumaga celebrations. This added a welcome break from work for feasting, dancing, and playing cricket.

Na uma lava na galuega na fai i uta, oi agai loan a galuega ki fale. Na fakaaoga e kimatou na koga na keli e Tony Atoni ke fai ai na tane o na tuku tua. Na aoga lele tenei avanoa ona kua kitea atu na itukaiga koga o te laukelekele, e mafai ai ke iloa na koga e tatau ke hukehuke kako heki kamata na kelikeliga.

Na manaia foki aua na mafai ke fakatahi kimatou i Atafu ite taimi na fai ai te Aho o te Mafutaga a Tina, fakatahi ai ma te Aho o te Aumaga, na mafai ai foki ke malololo mai na galuega, kae ke fakatahi ki na kaiga, na hiva ma na kilikiti.

photo: Adam Thompson

photo: *Rintaro Ono*

RESULTS FROM ATAFU AUGUST 2008 FIELDWORK

Rintaro talked with fishermen about their fishing methods. He quickly learned that the Atafu community of Wellington made an excellent book about Atafu traditional fishing methods. So there is no point for him to duplicate that work.

NA MEA NA MAUA MAI I NA GALUEGA NA FAKATINO I ATAFU ITE 2008

Na talanoa ia Dr.Ono ma na tautai, i na metotia e fakaaoga e kilatou i na faiva. Na iloa mai foki e ia ko na tamana Atafu mai Porirua- Ueligitone na fai he latou tuhi e fakatatau kina faiva o Atafu. Na mafaufau ai ia Dr.Ono e he aoga oi toe fai ni ana galuega agai kite faiga o na faiva.

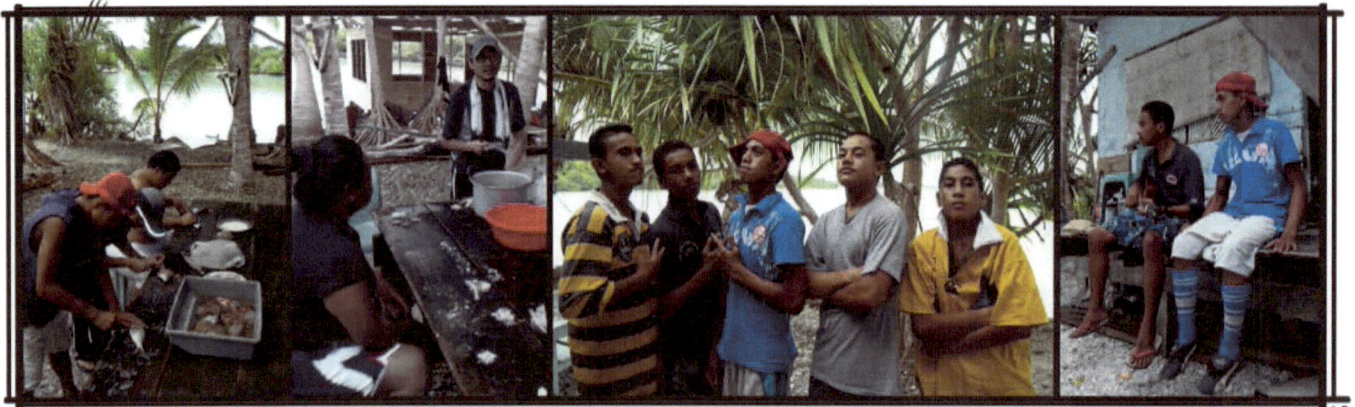

photos: *Bryon Bass, Timali Pele, Adam Thompson, and Rintaro Ono*

Rintaro spent most of his time catching fish and then turning the fish into clean and dry bones. Because he identifies fish from their bones, it is important for him to have a reference collection made from known fish specimens. So every fish was photographed and identified to species. Then they were carefully processed to take all of the soft parts off of the bones. Luckily, Rintaro had a good crew of students to help him while they also learned about his research.

Te lahiga la ote taimi o Dr. Ono na faka fano kite hakiliga o na itukaiga ika ma fai ai e ia na ika kae ke maua o latou pogaivi. Ona kote galuega a Dr. Ono, kote iloa ona ika mai o latou pogaivi, na taua lele ke fakaputu ma fakamaumau e ia na itukaiga ika i Atafu. Ko na ika uma la, na tapuke o latou ata, ma fakavahega pe ko nia na itukaiga ika ienei. Na fai la na galuega kiei, na kave kehe ai na kanofi kae ke maua mai na pogaivi. Na manaia foki na galuega ona na maua foki ni tamaiti aoga mai te aoga a Matauala ke fehoahoani ki na galuega.

photo: Rintaro Ono

photo: Timothy Gallaher

PLANTS AND TERRESTRIAL RESOURCE MANAGEMENT

Tim spent most of his time visiting with the people of Atafu. He spoke with them about the resources that they use and observed the resources that they harvested from the environment. Tim focused on the most useful food plants of Atafu, particularly Fala, Ulu, Niu, and Pulaka.

Fala and Pulaka in particular are very interesting since they are not very important food plants on volcanic islands, but appear to be very important on atolls. Tim interviewed people and conducted a survey to learn how the people of Atafu recognize diversity in these plants. He hopes to use this information to understand why there were so many names given by the people of Tokelau to different varieties of these species of plants and to understand the role of these varieties in ensuring that past generations of Tokelauans had enough resources to meet their needs over long periods of time.

NA LIHOHI I TE LAUKELEKELE MA TE TAI

Ko Tim na lahi mafuta ma tagata o Atafu. Nae talatalanoa kiei i na lihohi e fakaaoga i to latou hikomaga. Na lahi kikila agai kina lakau pito hili ona fakaaoga e Atafu, e veia kote fala, ulu, niu ma te pulaka.

Ko te pulaka ma te fala nae lahi kikila foki ki ei, ona kona lakau ienei e he lahi ona fakaaoga e tagata i na fenua ieia e fau i na mauga mu, kae taua ma fakaaoga ina fenua e ve Tokelau. Na talatalanoa ia Tim ma na tino, na fai foki ana fakamaumauga, ke ia iloa ai, pe vefea ona iloa e na tino Atafu te kehekehega in itukaiga lakau ienei. Fakatakitakiga, pe vefea ona iloa e te tino, na itukaiga fala kehekehe. E fia fakaaoga ienei fakamaumauga, ke iloa ai pe hea tena lahi venei ai ni igoa na kavea ki ienei itukaiga lakau, ma iloa te taua o ienei itukaiga lakau. Tona uiga, pe nae lahi, nae mautinoa ai nae lava na lihohi mo ona tagata ke ola ai mo ni piliota mataloa.

One other aspect of this work will be to understand how these plants and their associated cultivation and management practices have traveled throughout the Pacific. By comparing the names, legends and management practices for the plants of Tokelau to those of other island groups, we can learn about how these plants are connected. This may also give us some idea of how the people of Tokelau are connected with people in other atoll groups. In addition to what we learn from plant names, legends, and management practices, the DNA of these plants may also help us to learn how these important plants of Tokelau are connected to those on other islands.

It is well known that the times are changing for the people of Tokelau, as they are for people around the world. Traditions that have endured for many generations are giving way to modern practices imported from other countries. Tim hopes that by documenting some of the resource management traditions of Tokelau that this knowledge, built by generations of experience, will not be lost and can be carried into the future by the new generations of Tokelauans.

Ko te tahi vaega e fia maua mai i na galuega ienei e fai, kote malamalama pe na vefea ona pa ienei itukaiga lakau, ma ona auala e toto ma pulepule ai ki ietahi koga ote Pahefika. Kafai e fakatuhatuha e kitatou na igoa, ma na tala kakai ma na faiga ma pulepulega ki na lakau o Tokelau ki na tahi fenua ote Pahefika, e kitatou iloa na hokotaga o na lakau ienei. E mafai ai foki ke fakailoa mai ai, pe vefea ona hokotaga ia Tokelau ki ietahi fenua ote Pahefika. E he gata i na tala e maua mai i na igoa o na lakau, ma na tala kakai, ma na itukaiga pulepulega nae fai, ko na DNA o na lakau e fehoahoani foki ke iloa ai na hokotaga ki na tahi lakau i na tahi fenua.

photo: David Funk

ARCHAEOLOGICAL SURVEY

After walking over many kilometres of uta, we found that there is very little indication of archaeology on the ground surface. We only found a couple of graves and a few house foundations.

In order to see if we might be missing something under the surface, we did some small test excavations at Tuagafulu, Te Oki, and Laualalava. No subsurface cultural deposits were found on these three motus.

We concluded that the ancient pattern of settlement was probably similar to that of today, with people living permanently only on Fale, with uta used for resources and only temporary habitation.

NA FAKAMAUMAUAGA FAKA AKELOHI

Na lahi lele na kilomita na havavali ai kimatou i uta, na kimatou kitea ai foki nae he lahi ni vaega e mafai ke hukehuke ki ei i l luga ote laukelekele. E fia oi oti ia tugamau ma ni paepae o ni fale na maua e kimatou.

Na iei na tama galuega na fai e kimatou i uta, aua na iei he mea e he kitea e kimatou, na fai a matou galuega i te Tuagafulu, Te Oki, ma te Laualalava. Na heki maua e kimatou ni mea e fakamaonia ai na nofoia e tagata na fenua ienei.

Na iei la te lagona, ko na tino nae aumau ma nonofo lava i fale, ite mea e iei ai na tino ite taimi nei, kako uta nae fakaaoga lava ke kaumai ai na lihohi nae manakomia, ma tafafao kiei na tino mo ni taimi pukupuku.

ARCHAEOLOGICAL EXCAVATION

We excavated at three locations: TU-1 was at Pua and Poni Simi's house; TU-2 was at Penina and Vasefenua Reupena's house; and TU-3 was at Mili and Fano Fao's house.

HUKEHUKEGA FAKA AKELOHI KI LALO O TE KELEKELE

Na tolu ia koga na fai ai a matou galuega, kote vaega e takua ko TU-1 ite fale o Pua ma Poni Simi, TU-2 ite fale o Penina ma Vasefenu Reupena, ma TU-3 ite fale o Mili ma Fano Fao.

photo: Timothy Gallaher

TU-1

Test Unit 1 was the deepest that we excavated. The bottom of the earliest cultural layer is about 160 cm below the current ground surface. There are at least seven different cultural layers. Under the earliest cultural layer is a natural beach deposit with no signs of humans.

TU-1

Ko te koga tenei na maualalo ai a matou hukehukega. Ko te koga na maua ai e kimatou te vaega na nofoia muamua e katoa te 160 senitimita mai luga. E venei pe fitu ia koga kehekehe na nofoia e tagata. I lalo atu o te koga na nofoia e tagata muamua ko te matafaga, e heai foki ni vaega e iei e fakamaonia ai nae iei ni tino i te piliota tena.

Below: Profile of TU-1. Drawn by Tuipuavai Tago.

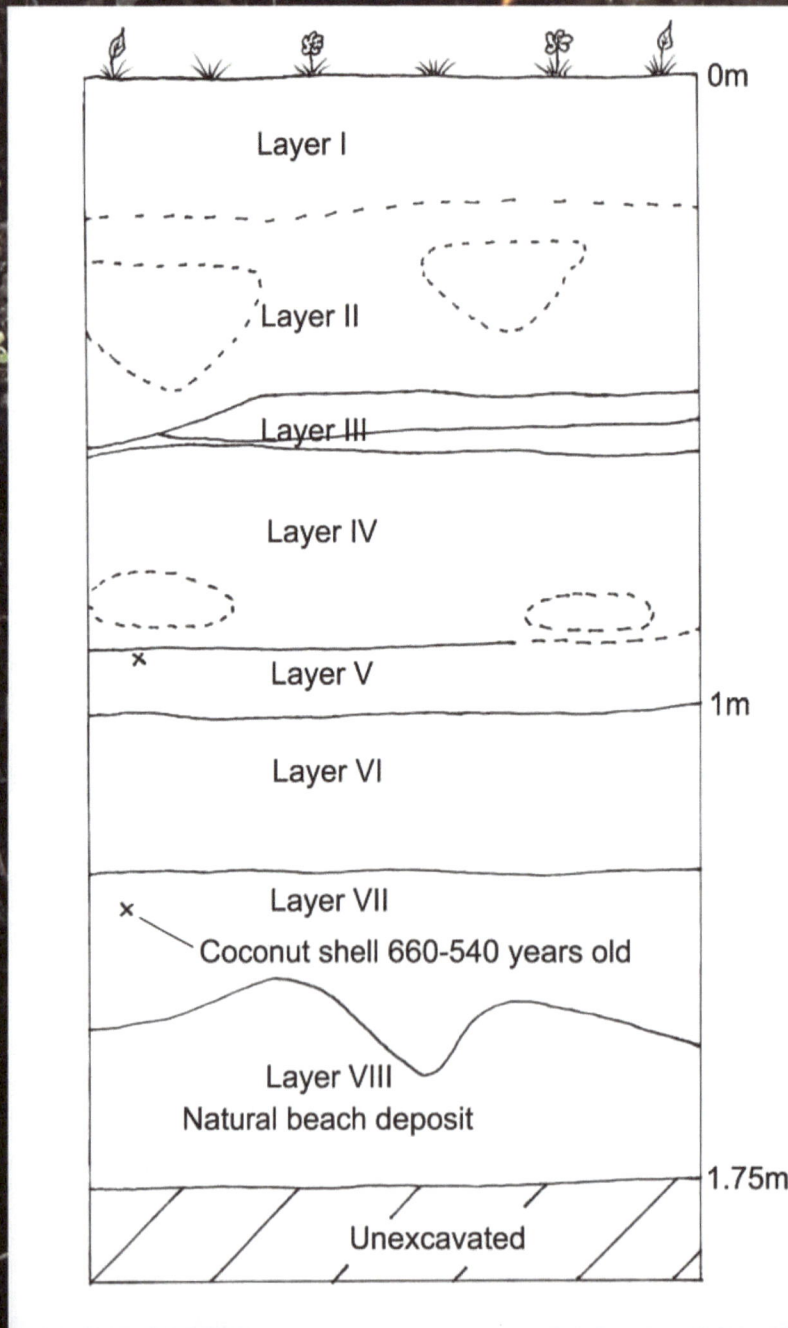

photo: Rintaro Ono

Above: Fish, pig, and chicken bones from TU-1. Note basalt umu rock on far left.

What we found when we started excavating was lots of charcoal and fish bone and pig bone and sheep bone. Also there were basalt umu rocks and palagi things like metal and glass. Because of the metal and glass, we knew that the top cultural layer wasn't that old. Also, when the first palagi came to Tokelau they didn't see any pigs, so we know that if there are pig bones in a cultural deposit, it must date to the time after palagi discovered Tokelau.

Basalt is a volcanic rock that doesn't occur naturally in Tokelau, so it had to be brought form outside. People bring bags of umu rocks today from Samoa, so it wasn't surprising to find them in the relatively new cultural deposit.

I te taimi na kamata ai na galuega na lahi lele a matou malala na maua, fakatahi ai ma na pogaivi ona ika, ma na pogaivi ona mamoe. Nae iei foki na fatu mai na mauga mu, ma na mea papalagi e veia kona ukamea ma na tioata. Ona na maua na mea papalagi, na kimatou iloa ko te koga tenei e he he koga kua mataloa atu. E kitatou iloa foki kote palagi na taunuku muamua ki Tokelau, e heki ia kitea ni pua, tona uiga kafai e maua ni pogaivi pua i he koga kelekele, e tatau ke hula ite taimi kua uma ai te taunuku o papalagi ki Tokelau.

Ko na fatu mauga mu e he ni fatu e tutupu faka te natula i Tokelau, tona uiga ko ni mea na kaumai i fafo atu o Tokelau. E lahi lele na fatu fai umu a na tino e kaumai i na aho nei mai Samoa, ko teia na mau ai e kimatou na fatu ienei i na koga o te laukelekele i luga. Kana lahi lele te huiga i te taimi kua agai ai lava kina koga i lalo. Kua kamata hui na mea e maua, nae maua pea lava na pogaivi o na

But then lower down, the deposit quickly changed. We continued to get fish bones but no more pig and sheep. These changes indicate a more traditional deposit. Interestingly, there continued to be basalt umu rocks. We started to think that maybe ancient people of Tokelau were bringing umu rock from high islands, just like people do today.

When we excavated farther down we had a real shock. We found dog bones and teeth. Everyone knows there are no dogs in Tokelau, and even the first palagi visitors saw no dogs. But in ancient times people raised dogs in Tokelau. We continued to get more basalt umu rocks and even basalt tool fragments. Just like the umu rocks, the basalt tools had to be brought from a high island.

This pattern continued all the way to the earliest cultural layer. Fish and dog bone and basalt tools fragments and umu rocks. What we can say now is that the very first people living at this site had contact with high islands.

ika, kae kua heai ni pua ma ni mamoe. Nae maua pea lava na fatu mauga mu, nae iei la na lagona pe ko nei ko na tino Tokelau i na aho ie kua leva nae kaumai foki e kilatou ni fatu fai umu e ve ko na Tokelau i na aho nei.

Na tekia lele kimatou kae koi agai lava kina koga i lalo. Na maua e kimatou na pogaivi maile ma ni nifo maile. E iloa uma e tagata e heai ni maile i Tokelau, ke pa foki kite papalagi na muamua mai ki Tokelau e heki ia kitea ni maile. Kae teia e kitatou kitea i na aho kua leva, ko na tino Tokelau nae tauhi e kilatou na maile. Nae maua pea lava a matou fatu umu ma ni kope e fai mai i na fatu mai na mauga mu. E veia lava ko na fatu mo na umu, ko na fatu foki ienei mo na kope e mautinoa na kauimai i fafo. Nae venei lava te tulaga nae iei te matou galuega nae fai ke pa lava kite koga na nofoia muamua.

E fokotahi te mea na kave ke hukehuke mo he tauhaga mai te koga nae nofoia muamua e tagata, na maua kua 600 kite 540 tauhaga kua teka. Ko te mea tenei na fakaaoga ko he ipu popo, ona e kitaou iloa he lakau e fakaaoga e tagata.

photo: Bryon Bass

Atmospheric data from Reimer et al (2004);OxCal v3.10 Bronk Ramsey (2005); cub r:5 sd:12 prob usp[chron]

WK-24478 TU-1 : 616±30BP

68.2% probability
1295AD (27.9%) 1330AD
1340AD (27.0%) 1370AD
1380AD (13.3%) 1395AD
95.4% probability
1290AD (95.4%) 1410AD

Atmospheric data from Reimer et al (2004);OxCal v3.10 Bronk Ramsey (2005); cub r:5 sd:12 prob usp[chron]

WK-24479 TU-2 359±30BP

WK-24478 TU-1 616±30BP

NZ7462 1000±100BP

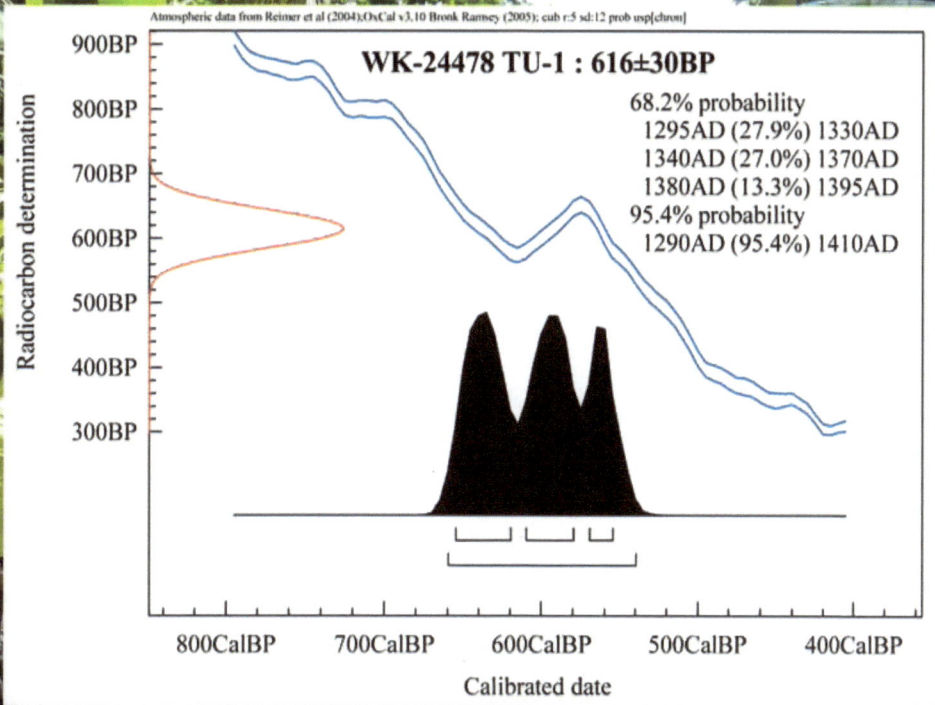

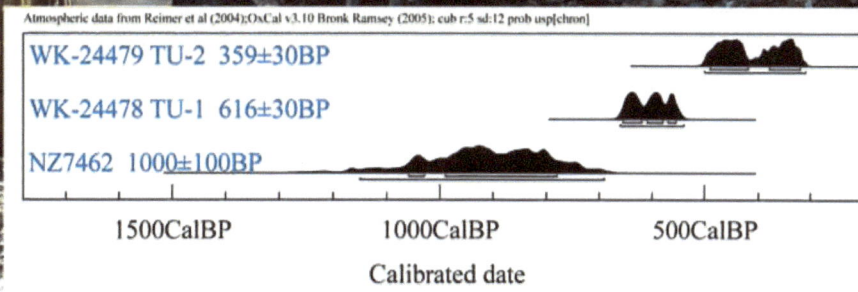

Above Top: Radiocarbon date from coconut shell charcoal in Layer VII of TU-1.
Above Bottom: Comparison of radiocarbon dates from TU-1, TU-2, and Simon Best's Atafu excavation. "BP" mean years Before Present.

One radiocarbon date was submitted from the lowest cultural layer. This date (WK-24478) has a radiocarbon age of 616±30 radiocarbon years. This means a calendar age of somewhere between 660-540 years ago. This sample was a piece of coconut shell, so we know that it was a human used plant.

This might help resolve the question of when people first settled in Tokelau. Simon Best found a date of 1200-700 years ago for the earliest cultural layer he found on Atafu. And on Fakaofo he found a date of 800-500 years ago for the earliest cultural deposit.

Although all of these dates have different ranges we can line them all up on a graph and see where they overlap. Perhaps, the place where they overlap is a good starting estimate for the actual date when people first arrived in Tokelau.

Atonu e mafai te vaega tenei ke fehoahoani kite fehili pe ko anafea tena omamai ai na tino ki Tokelau. I na hukehukega a Simon Best na maua ana tauhaga mo te koga na nofoia e tagata muamua mai te 1200 kite 700 tauhaga kua teka mo Atafu. I Fakaofo, na maua ana tauhaga mai te 800 kite 500 tauhaga kua teka, mo te koga na nofoia muamua e tagata.

Atonu kona tauhaga ienei kua tuku atu e kehekehe, e mafai ke tuku e kitatou ki luga o he kalafa, ke kikila kitatou kiei. Hove ko te koga e iei ai ai he hokotaga o na tauhaga e tolu ienei, ko te tauhaga tonu tena na nofoia ai ia Tokelau.

TU-2

Test Unit 2 was located near the lagoon shore, on the inland side of Penina and Vase's house. The lowest cultural deposit at this excavation ended at about 125 cm below the current ground surface. The stratigraphy at this excavation was very different from TU-1. In TU-2 there is one main cultural layer. Although it must have been deposited over some centuries, we could not distinguish different layers. The cultural layer has so much charcoal in it, that it looks black.

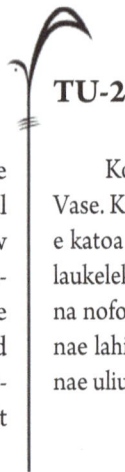

TU-2

Ko te TU-2 nae tu ite pito ki namo, ite tafa fale o Penina ma Vase. Ko te vaega na maua ai te koga muamua na nofoia e ni tino e katoa te 125 senitimita mai luga. Nae kehekehe na koga o te laukelekele i kinei ma TU-1. I te TU-2, e fokotahi lava te koga ve na nofoia e tagata, nae he kitea ni tahi koga na nofoia e ni tino, nae lahi lele na malala na maua, ko te lahiga o te koga kelekele nae uliuli.

Below: Profile of TU-2. Drawn by Tuipuavai Tago.

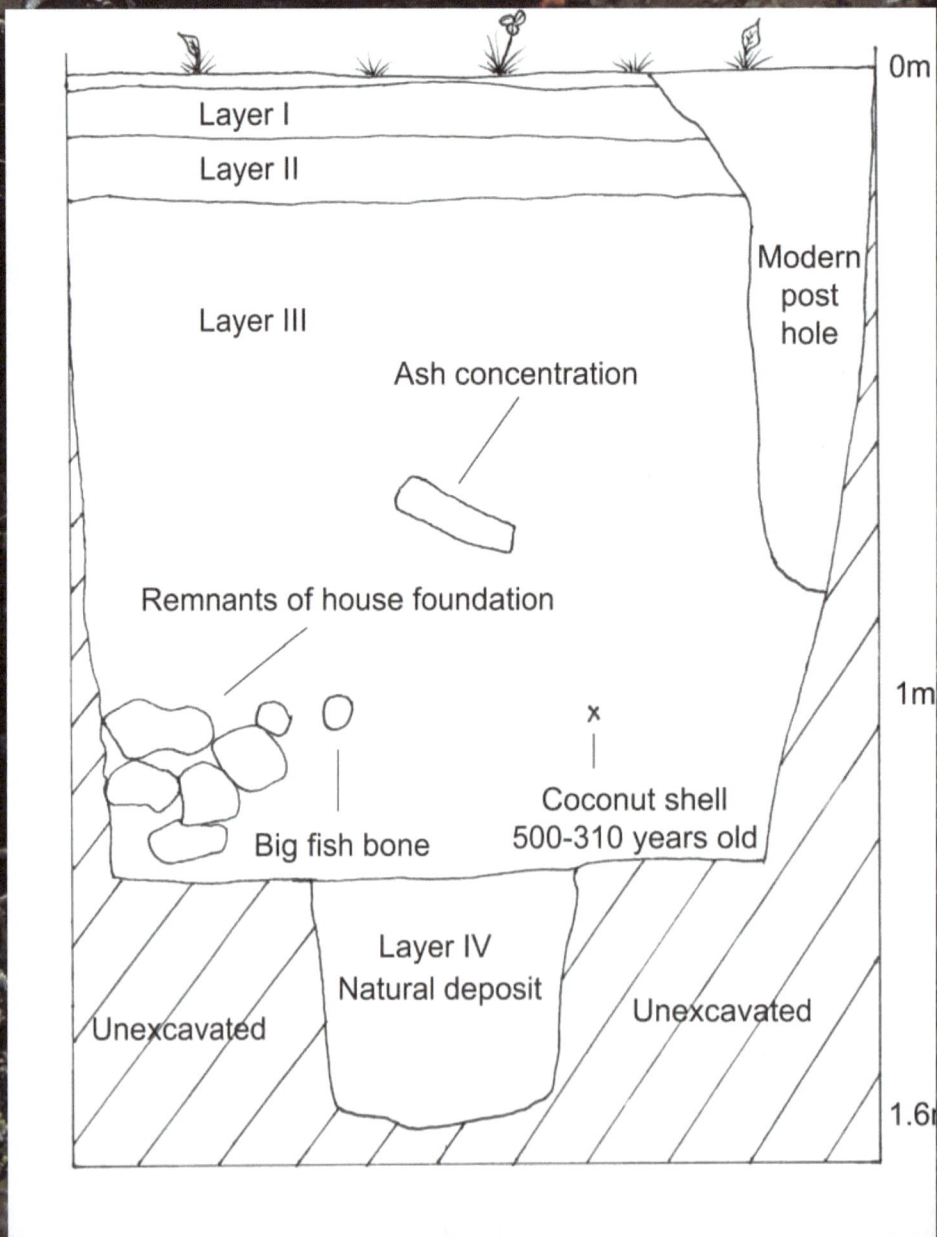

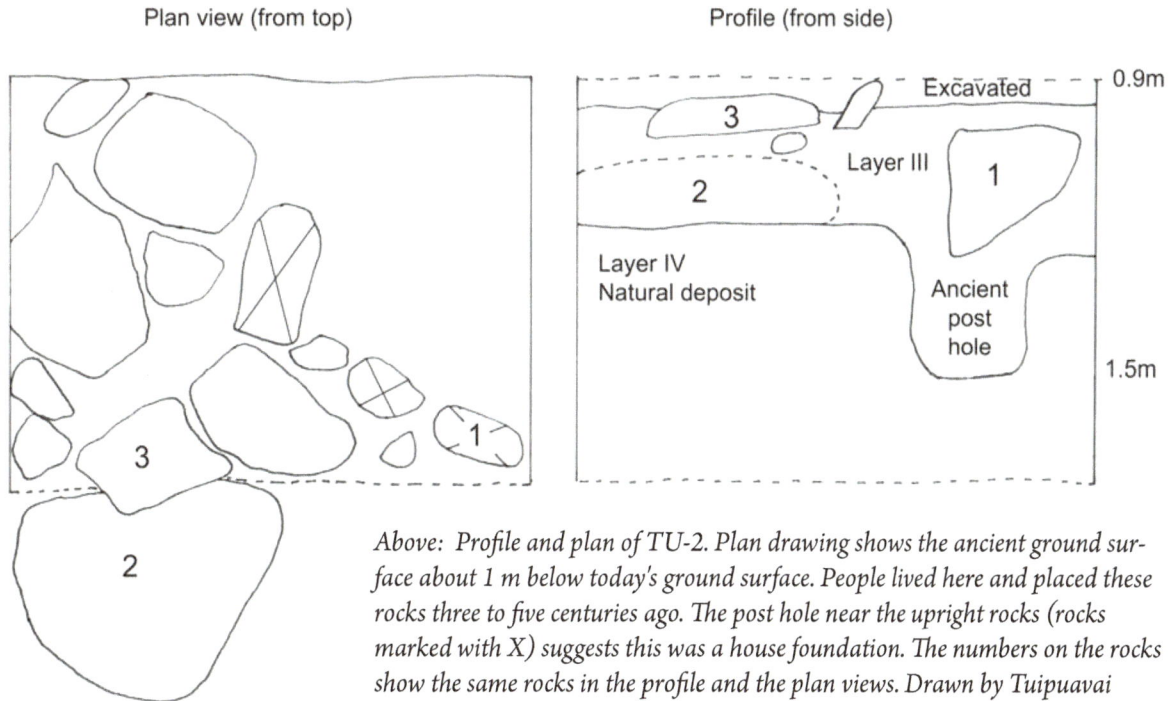

Plan view (from top)

Profile (from side)

Excavated — 0.9m

Layer III

Layer IV
Natural deposit

Ancient
post
hole

1.5m

Above: Profile and plan of TU-2. Plan drawing shows the ancient ground surface about 1 m below today's ground surface. People lived here and placed these rocks three to five centuries ago. The post hole near the upright rocks (rocks marked with X) suggests this was a house foundation. The numbers on the rocks show the same rocks in the profile and the plan views. Drawn by Tuipuavai Tago.

The cultural material from TU-2 was similar to TU-1. Lots of fish and dog bone, basalt tool fragments and umu rocks, and also some broken piece of fishhooks made from pearl shell (tifa).

The very interesting thing that we found in TU-2 was what appears to be an ancient house foundation. This is made of thin coral rocks standing on the edges in a line and lots of smaller coral rocks around them filling up the space. These rocks are placed directly on a natural beach deposit.

Ko na mea nae maua ite TU-2nae tutuha kina mea nae maua i te TU-1. Nae lahi na pogaivi ona ika ma na maile, ma na fatu e fau ai na kope ma fai umu, nae iei foki na matau e fau mai na tifa.

Ko te tahi vaega taua na maua e kimatou ite TU-2, e ve ko ni paepae o he fale i na aho kua leva. E fau mai ina fatu papa manifinifi lele, e fakatutu fakatahi i he laina, kae fola i ni kilikili. I lalo ifo o na paepae fatu ienei, kote matafaga.

Below: Polynesian rat (Rattus exulans) bones from TU-2

Atmospheric data from Reimer et al (2004);OxCal v3.10 Bronk Ramsey (2005); cub r:5 sd:12 prob usp[chron]

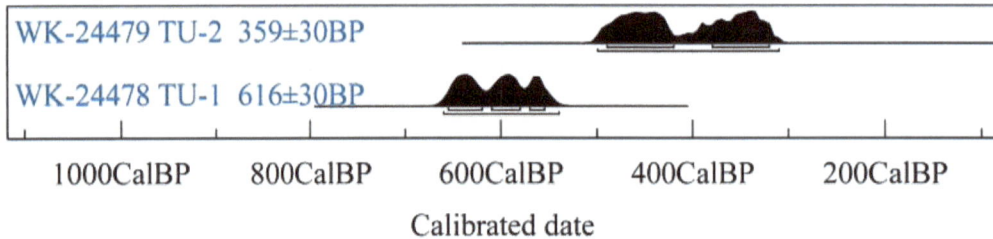

WK-24479 TU-2 359±30BP

WK-24478 TU-1 616±30BP

| 1000CalBP | 800CalBP | 600CalBP | 400CalBP | 200CalBP |

Calibrated date

Above: Comparison of radiocarbon dates from TU-1 and TU-2.

We took a piece of coconut shell (WK-24479) from the top of this rock pavement. This date has a radiocarbon age of 359±30 radiocarbon years. This means a calendar age of somewhere between 500-310 years ago. Although we don't know the exact date the house foundation was built, we do know that the date ranges from TU-1 and TU-2 do not overlap. This tells us that the building of the house foundation in TU-2 was sometime after the earliest cultural deposit in TU-1.

Team member Dr. Jennifer Kahn from the Bishop Museum in Hawai'i is a specialist in excavating ancient houses in Polynesia. She will be able to understand things about ancient household life in Tokelau by studying ancient house sites like the one found in TU-2.

Na kave e kimatou he ipu popo nae tatia i luga ote paepae fatu tenei. Na maua mai te tauhaga o tenei koga mai te 500 kite 310 tauhaga kua teka. Atonu e he maua tonu te tauhaga na fau ai te paepae fale tenei, kako te mea e mautinoa e he feta, pe iei ni kehekehega kafai e faka tuha kina tauhaga na maua mai i te TU-1. Tona uiga e kitatou iloa e heki mataloa te iei ona tino ite TU-2 kae fai loa te paepae ote fale.

Te tahi tino o tenei polokalame, ia Dr Jennifer Kahn mai te Bishop Museum i Hawai'i, he tino e hukehuke kina fale o tagata Polenisia i na aho kua leva. Atonu e malamalama atili kitatou kina itukaiga nofonofoga i na kaiga e auala mai ite hukehuke o na vaega ve na maua ite TU-2.

photo: Timothy Gallaher

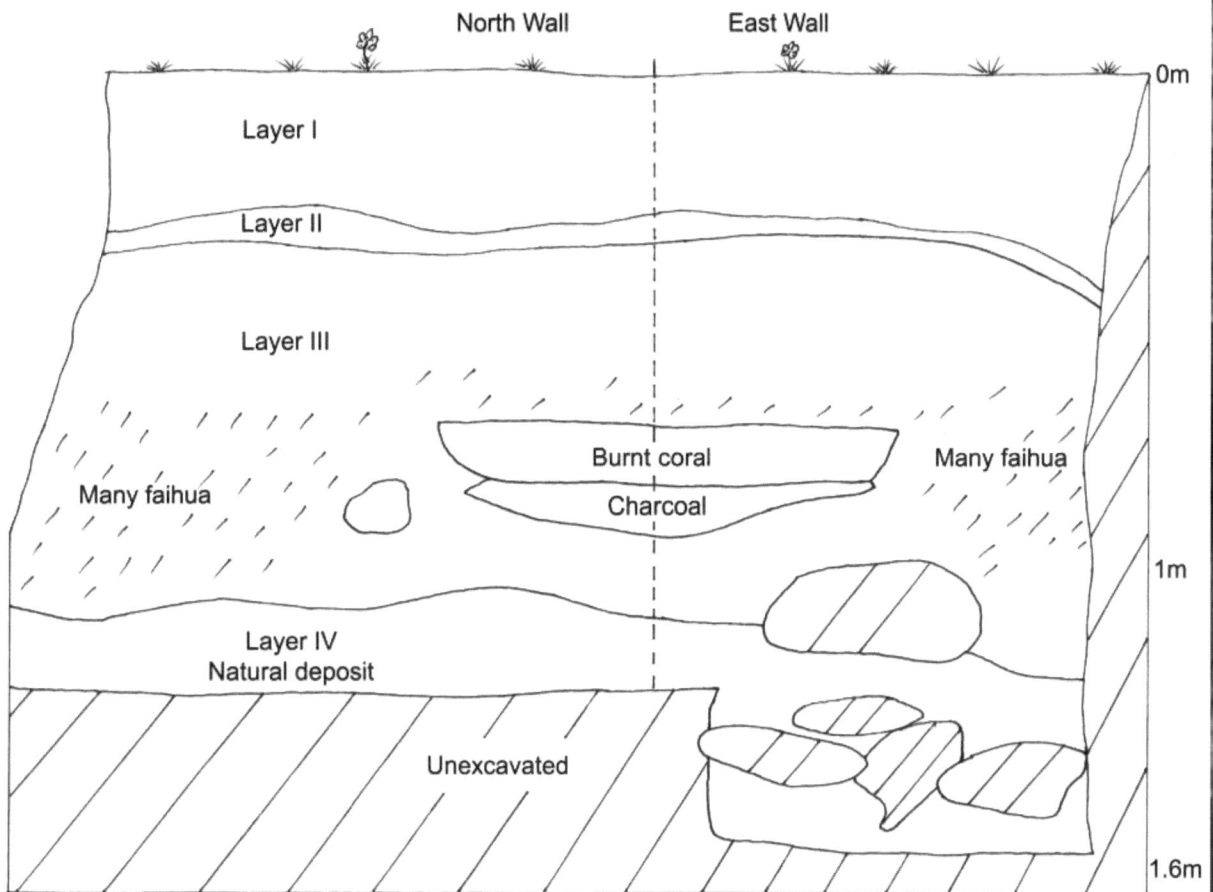

Above: Profile of two walls of TU-3. Drawn by Tuipuavai Tago. Dashed lines indicate area of dense faihua (Tridacna sp) shells.

In the figure:
North Wall, East Wall, 0m, Layer I, Layer II, Layer III, Burnt coral, Charcoal, Many faihua, Many faihua, 1m, Layer IV Natural deposit, Unexcavated, 1.6m

TU-3

Test Unit 3 was also located near the beach, on the side of Mili and Fano's house. Again, the stratigraphy here is different from the other excavations.

The lowest cultural layer ended at about 110 cm below the current ground surface. Just below this cultural deposit is the water table. The deposit was somewhat similar to TU-2, but there was very much less charcoal. This makes the deposit at TU-3 look more grey than black.

Two interesting things were found in the deposit at TU-3. One was a thick layer full of giant clam shells (faihua). The other is a fire feature that may have been used for burning coral or shell to make lime. No dating samples were processed from TU-3.

TU-3

E he mamao foki te koga tenei mai te matafaga

I te itu ki namo, ite tafa fale o Mili ma Fano. Ko te hukehukega foki o te koga kelekele e kehekehe ma te TU-1 ma te TU-2. Te koga na nofoia muamua e tagata na maua kite 110 senitimita mai luga. I lalo malie atu ote koga tenei kote tai. Ko na mea na maua e taii tutuha kina mea na maua ite TU-2, kae nae he lahi te malala. Nae ve e lanu kekefu, kae he uliuli.

Nae lua ia mea taua na maua ite TU-3. Te mea muamua ko te tahi koga na nofoia e tagata nae tumu i na fahua. Ko te tahi mea, e ve ko he mea e tai ve he oga uma nae fakaaoga ke huhunu ai ni figota. E heki maua ni tauhaga mo na mea na maua mai ite TU-3.

PLANS FOR THE FUTURE

The initial results from Atafu are very encouraging. We have found very good cultural deposits that can help answer some of the key questions about Tokelau's ancient past.

Samples of dog, rat, and chicken bone have been sent to Dr. Matisoo-Smith for DNA analysis. Professor Peter Mills and Dr. Steve Lundblad are doing geochemical analysis of the basalt tool fragments we found in August. Dr. Ono is working on identifying the fish remains form the excavations. We eagerly await the results of these analyses and clues they can provide about Tokelau's past.

The August research on Atafu was just a small start. Because of funding limits only a small team could come from outside. In 2009 we hope to have more funding to continue working on Atafu with the full team of scientists. Then, pending the availability of funding, we look forward to taking the project to Nukunonu and Fakaofo in 2010 and 2011.

PELENI MO TE LUMANAKI

Ko na mea kua maua mai i na galuega kua fai i Atafu e manaia lele mo te agai pea ki mua. E iei na koga kelekele e lahi ai ni vaega e mafai ke kaumai ai ni vaega e mafai ke tali ai na fehili agai kite olaga ona tino Tokelau i na aho kua leva.

E iei na mea e ve ko na pogaivi o na kimoa, maile, ma na moa kua kave kia Dr. Lisa Martisoo Smith ke hukehuke o latou DNA. Ko Professor Peter Mills ma Dr Steve Lundblad e hukehuke e kilau na kope ieia e fau mai i na fatu mai na mauga mu. Ko Dr.Ono, e fakamaumau e ia na pogaivi ika na maua mai ina galuega na fai. Kua lahi lele te fofou kei na uma tenei vaega, kae ke maua mai ai foki ni a tatou tala agai ki Tokelau i na aho kua leva.

Ko te galuega na fai i Aukuho i Atafu, kohe tama kamataga, ona foki kona mea tau tupe e heki lahi he vaega na mafai ke fakatino, ma heki tokalahi ni tino na mafai ke omai i fafo. E talohia e lava he fakatupega ite 2009, kae ke fakaauau na galuega i Atafu, ma katoa uma na haienitihi. E ve ia foki lava na fakamoemoe mo te tapena atu ki te taimi kua meki ai te polokalame ki Nukunonu ma Fakaofo ite tauhaga 2010 ma te 2011.

photo: David Addison

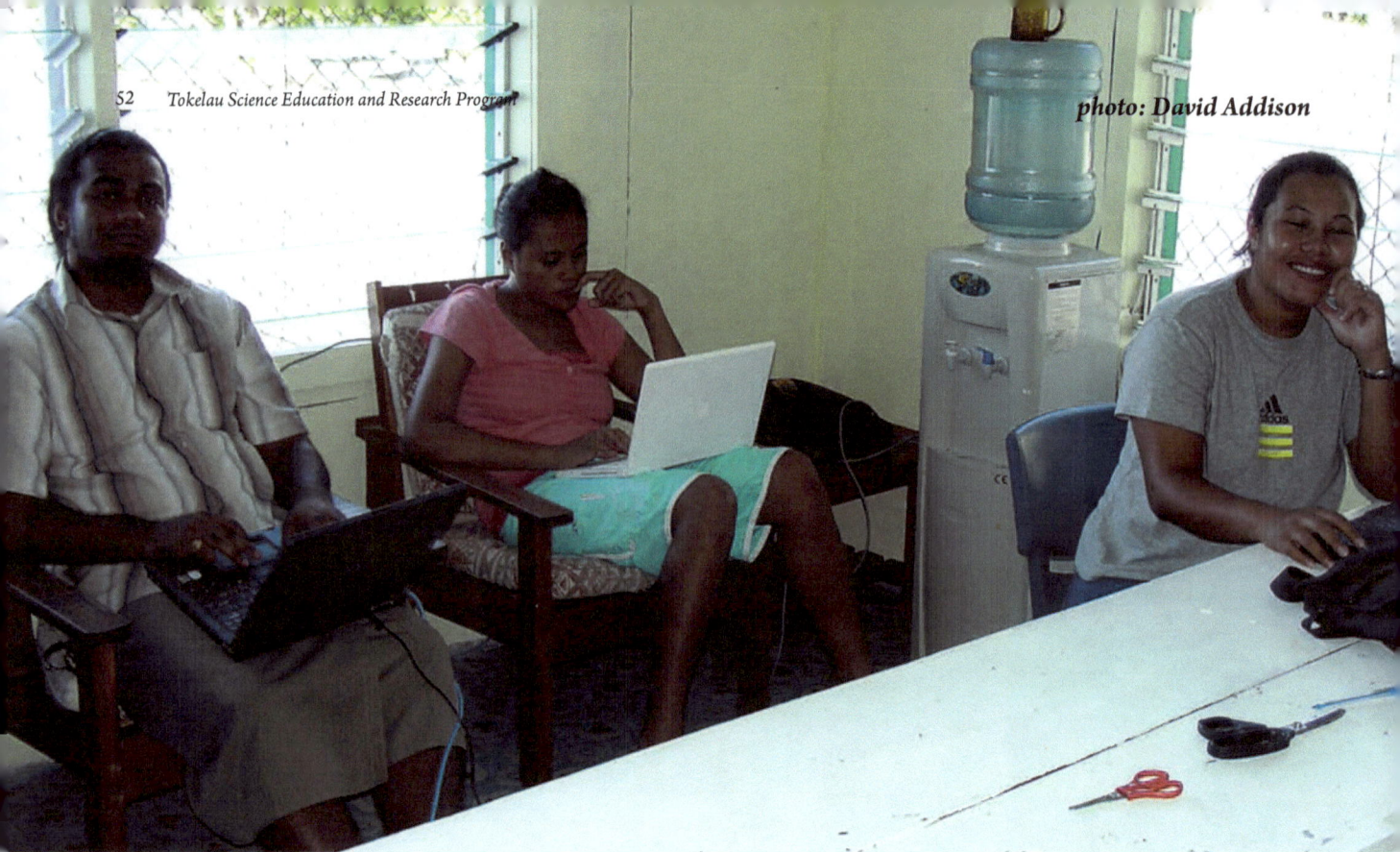

THANK YOU LETTERS

FROM GAIL AND DAVID FUNK

Thanks for making us feel so welcome. It was a treat for me to sing at the school and to try to dance with the children. We loved learning about cricket and sharing in the delicious feast at the men's festival. We remember with great fondness our short time on your atoll and hope to visit again.

Cheers, Gail & David on Fifth Season

NA TUHI FAKAFETAI

MAIA GAIL MA DAVID FUNK

E momoli atu te fakafetai mai te kimaua, ko au na fiafia lele na maua he avanoa ke pehe ai au ite aoga ma taumafai foki ke hihiva ma na tamaiti. Kimaua na fiafia lele na maua he avano ke akoakogia ai foki kimaua ite tafaoga kote kilikiti, ma fakatahi ite kaiga malie lele na fai ite Aho ote Aumaga. E manatua pea e kimaua te tama taimi na mafuta ai kitatou i Atafu, ma fakamoemoe e toe feiloaki kitatou i he aho.

Fakafetai maia Gail ma David Funk ote 5th Season

FROM TIMOTHY GALLAHER

I would like to thank you, the people of Atafu, for your kind generosity and the wonderful welcome that you gave us during our short stay on your island. I enjoyed learning from you and living with you and I hope that we will soon be together again. I will carry with me many fond memories of your stories and songs, of playing cricket, and just being with you and living with you. I only regret that I did not have more time to get to know each of you better during my stay. Also, if in my ignorance I caused offence to anyone I am sorry.

Until we meet again, Timothy Gallaher

MAIA TIMOTHY GALLAGHER

E fakafetai atu kia te koutou na tino o Atafu, ki te koutou alolofa mai i te tama taimi nae kina ai kimatou. Ko au na fiafia lele ina mea na akoako mai e koutou, ma toku mafuta ma koutou, ma fakamoemoe ko kitatou e toe mafuta ihe taimi pili mai. E kave e au ni mafaufauga aulelei ia koutou tala ma na pehe, ma te taimi nae tafao kilikiti ai au, ke pa lava kite tatou mafutaga. Ko te mea lava na napa ai au, e heki lava he taimi ke ko iloa uma ai koutou ite taimi nae kina ai au. Kafai foki e iei he mea e heki manuia ite tatou mafutaga, fakamagalo mai au.

Ke toe feiloaki kitatou, Timothy Gallaher

photo: David Funk

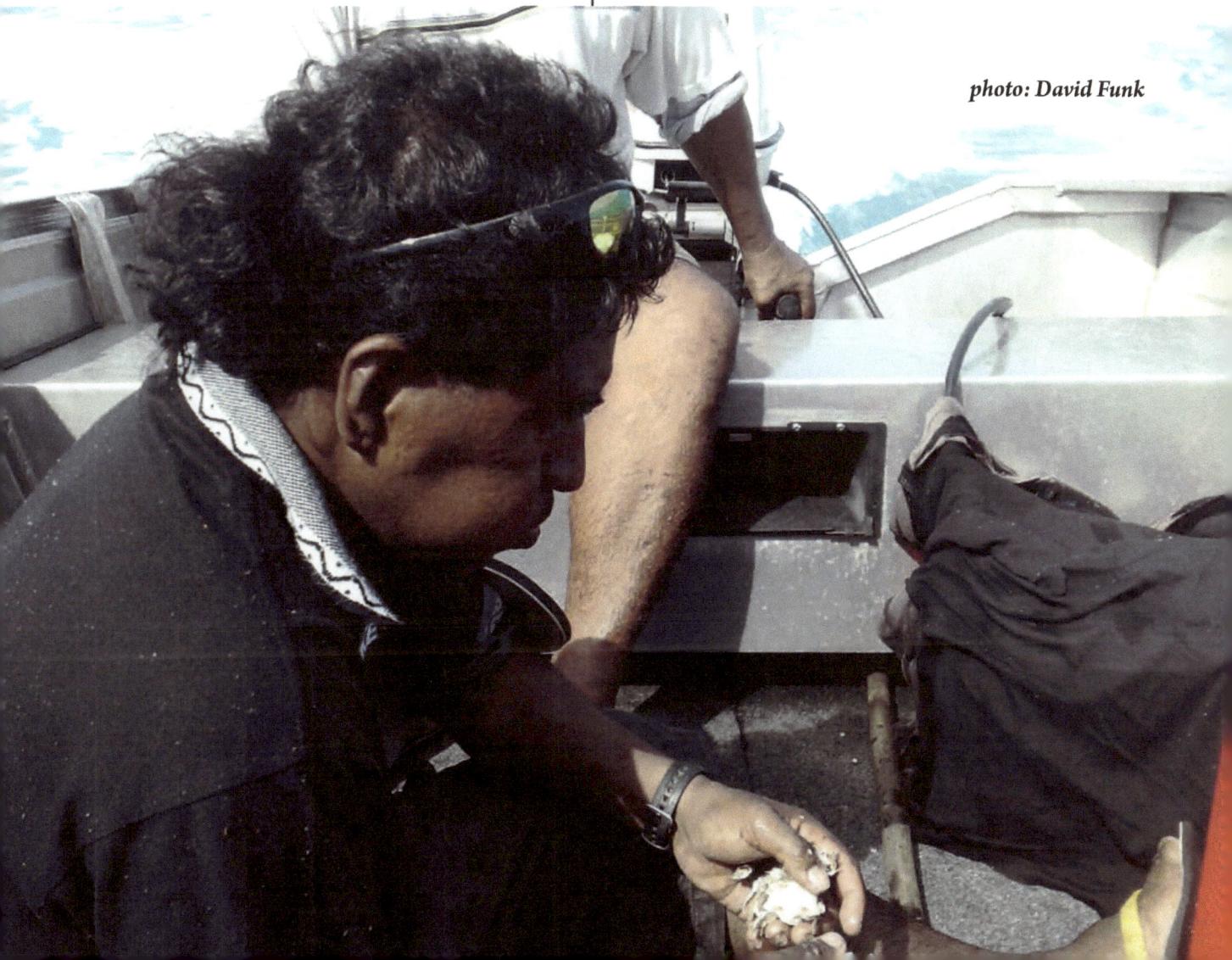

FROM RINTARO ONO

To my dear friends on Atafu,

I wish to express my best appreciation to everyone in Atafu, particularly for your warm friendship, understanding and support of our research and stay in Atafu. Although it is impossible to write all of your individual names here, I wish to thank all of our friends in Atafu and am looking forward to see you again soon!

Rintaro Ono

MAIA RINTARO ONO

Ki aku uo mamae i Atafu,

E momoli atu te fakafetaii ki tagata uma o Atafu, mo te fai uho, ma te lagolago ma malamalama ki te polokalame ma te matou nofo i Atafu. Atonu e he mafai ke tuhi uma o koutou igoa i kinei, kae e momoli atu te fakafetai lahi lele ki a matou uo i Atafu, ma toe fia kikila atu kite aho e toe feiloaki ai kitatou.

Rintaro Ono

photo: David Addison

photo: David Addison

FROM ADAM THOMPSON

To the People of Atafu,

Thank you for your hospitality. Your accommodation was most gracious and your island most beautiful. I look forward to returning to see all of your beautiful faces again and to enjoy your most excellent food. I hope we did not eat all of the coconut crab and some is left for you. I enjoyed most dancing in the Lotala during the festivities and hearing your songs and look forward to enjoying them again.

Sincerely, Adam Thompson

MAIA ADAM THOMPSON

Ki na tino o Atafu,

Fakafetai atu kite tauhiga o kimatou, ko te koutou fenua te aulelei. Ko au e fiafia lele ke fia toe liliu atu ma toe kikila atu ki o koutou foliga aulelei, ma kai foki ki a koutou meakai malie. Talohia e heki kai uma e kimatou a koutou ugauga, nae iei ni mea na faka totoe ma koutou. Ko au na fiafia lele kina pehe, ma na hiva na fai i Lotala, ma fia toe fakatahi atu ki ei.

Fakafeta, Adam Thompson

photo: David Addison

BRYON BASS

I'd like to thank the people of Atafu for their warmth, kindness, and generosity during our 2008 field research season. Thank you for allowing our team members into your world, and letting us become part of your daily lives! I hope to see you all again very soon!

Bryon

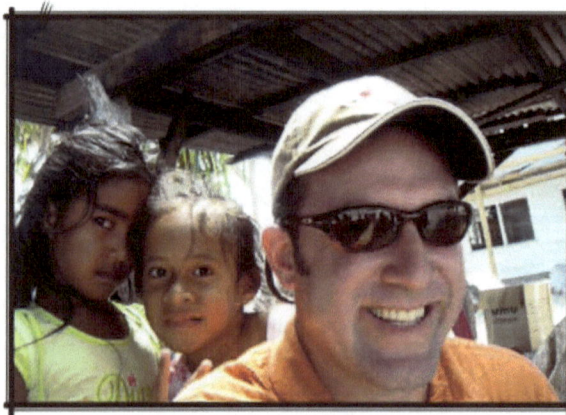

BRYON BASS

E momoli atu te fakafetai ki tagata o Atafu, mo to latou alolofa mai ite taimi na mafuta ai kimatou i na galuega na fai ite 2008. E fakafetai atu mote talia ote matou kau maulaga ki toutou lalolagi, ma kavea kimatou ma vaega o koutou olaga. E fakamoemoe ke toe feiloaki ma koutou uma ihe taimi pili mai.

Bryon

TIMALI PELE

Dear Taupulega and the people of Atafu,

It was truly an honor to meet such wonderful and generous people. The day we arrived to Atafu, peo-ple were so friendly and kind as we meet the people of Atafu. The feeling that got to me, it felt as if we arrived to our homeland and families, and I'm really thankful of this opportunity. Special thank you to the Taupulega for allowing our crew to conduct research in Atafu. To the Fatupaepae, thank you for the gifts and everything that was provided to our crew. I would also like to thank the Pulenuku, and the Aumaga for assisting us around the village. Special thanks to Dr. Lameka and the Tonuia family for opening their doors to our crew when we arrived in Atafu. I hope our project was helpful to the people and especially the younger generation of Atafu. God bless Atafu, and God bless Tokelau.

Timali Pele

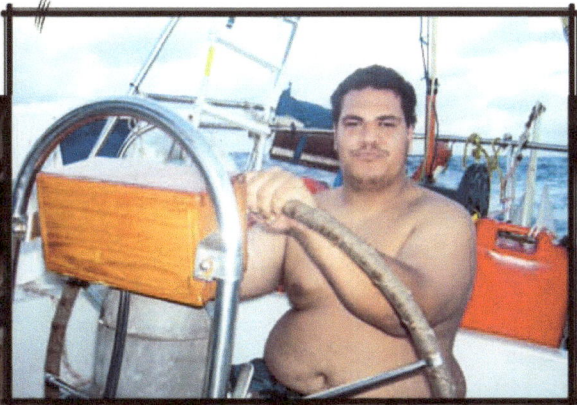

TIMALI PELE

Kite Taupulega ma tagata o Atafu,

E fakafetai na maua he avanoa gali na mafai ai au ke feiloaki ma ni tino alolofa e ve ko koutou. I te aho na taunuku ai kimatou ki Atafu, te alolofa mai ona tino o Atafu. Na ko lagona, e ve lava ko au kua pa ki toku fenua ma toku kaiga, ma fakaftai au ki tenei avanoa. Fakafetai fakapito atu kite Taupulega mo te fakatagaga na foki mai ke fakatino ai tenei polokalame i Atafu. E fakafetai atu foki kite Fatupaepae mo na meaalofa na foki mai kite kau Malaga, ma na mea uma. E fakafetai atu foki kite Pulenuku, ma te Aumaga mo te fehoahoani . E fakafetai fakapitoa foki kia Dr. Lameka Sale, fakatahi ai kite kaiga o Asora Tonuia mo te tatala mai o latou faitotoka mo te kau Malaga ite taimi kua taunuku atu ai ki Atafu. E fakamoemoe na lahi lele te fehoahoani ote polokalame ki tagata kae maihe te tupulaga talavou o Atafu. Ke fakamanuia atu te Atua kia te koutou uma, ma fakamanuia te Atua kia Tokelau.

Timali Pele

photo: Timothy Gallaher

MARIE FAATUALA

Malo Ni!

My stay in Tokelau was the most wonderful experience and the loveliest place I have ever visited and I want to thank you all for being so supportive and for accepting us in your village. I would like to take this opportunity to thank everybody who welcomed us in your village; your Tokelauan hospitality has proven to be a warm welcome for our team.

I want to thank John Kalolo and his wife's family, Ms.Haleika for your hospitality and please send my love to mama Nanaulu, Dr.Lameka and his family and for the usage of his residence, the Taupulega for accepting us in your presence and approving our research that we wanted to conduct. I also want to thank the Department of Education for allowing us to use their computers, their facility and for allow-ing us to talk to the students. Also I would like to thank Tene and Hale for being with us during our survey and the boat ride was awesome! Also to the telephone communications crew, Thank You! To anybody and everybody who has made our stay in Tokelau possible thank you from the bottom of my heart. Your kindness, support and generosity are one of a kind and I thank you all.

I also want to thank the elderly ladies; I have considered you all my grandmothers since I was the only girl on this trip. Your hospitality and your warm welcoming have touched my heart and I am ever so grateful, appreciative and thankful for accepting me and the team in open arms. I love all of you my Tokelauan Grandmothers, aunties and sisters for ever being so warm and kind at me, your name has escaped me but your love and kindness is never forgotten. Thank you for the gifts and it is an everyday reminder of your kindness, hospitality and love towards me.

Even though I stayed for only a week but the chance to visit and be a Tokelauan for a week has been a great and wonderful time and experience of my life. Words are not enough to express my gratitude but I thank you all.

Fakafetai ma fakamanuia atu le Atua i le tou Nu'u. (Thank you and God Bless Atafu and its citizens).

Marie Faatuala

MARIE FAATUALA

Malo Ni.

Na fatoa pa au kihe fenua e pito hili tona aulelei, e fakafetai atu ai au kite lagolago mai ma te talia o kimatou ite koutou fenua. E kavea tenei avanoa, e fakafetai ai au kia te koutou uma, ko toutou agaga tali malo alolofa faka Tokelau e takutino atu e au te mafanafana ko.

E fakafetai atu kia Asora Tonuia ma tona kaiga(i've changed John Kalolo to Asora's family,this is becos it i always culturally appropriate to mention the parent's names), e fakafetai atu foki kia Faleika Asora, mo tona alofa mai, vena kia Nana Fulu. E fakafetai atu kia Dr Lameka ma tona kaiga, mo te fakaavanoa mai o tona maota, vena ma te Taupulega mo te taliagia o kimatou ma te polokalame. E momoli atu foki te fakafetai kite Mataeke o Akoakoga, mo te fakaavanoa mai a latou mahini ma o latou potu, ma te avanoa ke feiloaki ki tamaiti aoga. E fakafetai atu foki kia Tene Aluia ma Hale Kalolo, mo te fakatai mai ite taimi ote polokalame, te manaia foki ite taimi e tiketike ai kimatou i na vaka. E fakafetai atu foki ki kaufaigaluega ate Mataeke o Hokotaga. Kae maihe mo tagata uma na alolofa mai ite matou nonofo i Atafu. E maua gata he agaga alofa vena e maua e koutou.

E fakafetai atu foki kina matua matutua, ko koutou kua ve lava ni tupuna e o au, ona foki ko au oi oti te tama fafine i tenei kaumalaga.

Na loga e au ite loto, toutou agalelei ma te alofa kite taliga o kimatou ite koutou fenua. E fakafetai atu ki fafine kua ve lava ko oku tupuna , kua ve lava ni uho o toku matua ma na uho o au. E fakafetai lahi lele foki mo na meaalofa. E tuha lava pena katoa oi toi toku vaiaho i Atafu, ko te avanoa ke fano ma nofo i Tokelau, e he toe mafai ke puli ai au. E talitonu e he lava ni kupu, e kavatu ai te lagona fakafetai, kae e toe fakafetai lahi lele atu kia te koutou.

Fakafetai ma fakamanuia atu te Atua ki te nuku katoa.

Marie Faatuala

ANN AND BARRY LANGE

Barry and I would like to express our sincere thanks for the opportunity of visiting and interacting with your community. We were very excited about becoming part of the archaeological expedition which took place in August, 2008. Upon our arrival in the community the friendship and helpfulness which was extended to us was overwhelming. I spent many hours sitting with an elder in her fare while she wove hats and mats, communicating with gestures and broken English. It was an experience I will never forget, mixing with people of another culture and sharing knowledge. I spoke to the children in school about my home, Canada, and I hope I opened their eyes to how people live there. We participated in two meetings with the elders and felt privileged to learn how the village governed itself. It was an opportunity of a lifetime to be allowed to land, visit and work in Atafu and one we will never forget. Thank you from the bottom of our hearts.

Ann and Barry Lange
S/V Cat's-Paw IV

ANN MA BARRY LANGE

E momoli atu te ma fakafetai ma Barry, mo te avanoa na mafai ai ke ahiahi atu ma feiloaki ma te koutou nuku. Kimaua nae fiafia lele na maua he avanoa ke fakatahi ai kite polokalame Akelohi teia na fai i Aukuho 2008.Na lahi lele te koutou fehoahoani, I te taimi na taunuku atu ai kimaua ki luga o Atafu. Na lahi lele toku taimi na mafuta ai au ma he matua matua i tona fale, ma matamata kite lalagaga o tana pulou ma tana moega. Ko te lomatua foki nae he lelei lahi ite gagana peletania, nae fakaaoga foki la ona lima ke fakataaga mai ai na mea nae talatalanoa ai kimaua. Ko te avanoa tenei na ko maua e he toe puli ia te au, he avanoa na feiloaki ai ma ni tino e kehe te latou aganuku ma mafai ke akoakoa ai ni ietahi iloa. Na talanoa au kina tamaiti aoga agai ki toku fenua ko Kanata, ma fakamoemoe na kilatou iloa foki te olaga ona tino e nonofo ai. Na lua a matou fakatahiga ma te Taupulega, ma ko au na fiafia lele, na ko iloa ai te itukaiga pulepulega ote fenua. Kimaua na fiafia lele, na maua he avanoa ke tau atu ai ki Atafu, na mafai foki ke ahiahi, fakatahi ai na mafai kimaua ke galulue ai, e he mafai ke toe puli ia te kimaua. E lagaona pea ite loto, te agaga fakafetai.

Ann ma Barry Lange
S/V Cat's Paw IV

photos on following pages by Timali Pele, Bryon Bass, Timothy Gallaher, David Funk, Rintaro Ono, and Adam Thompson

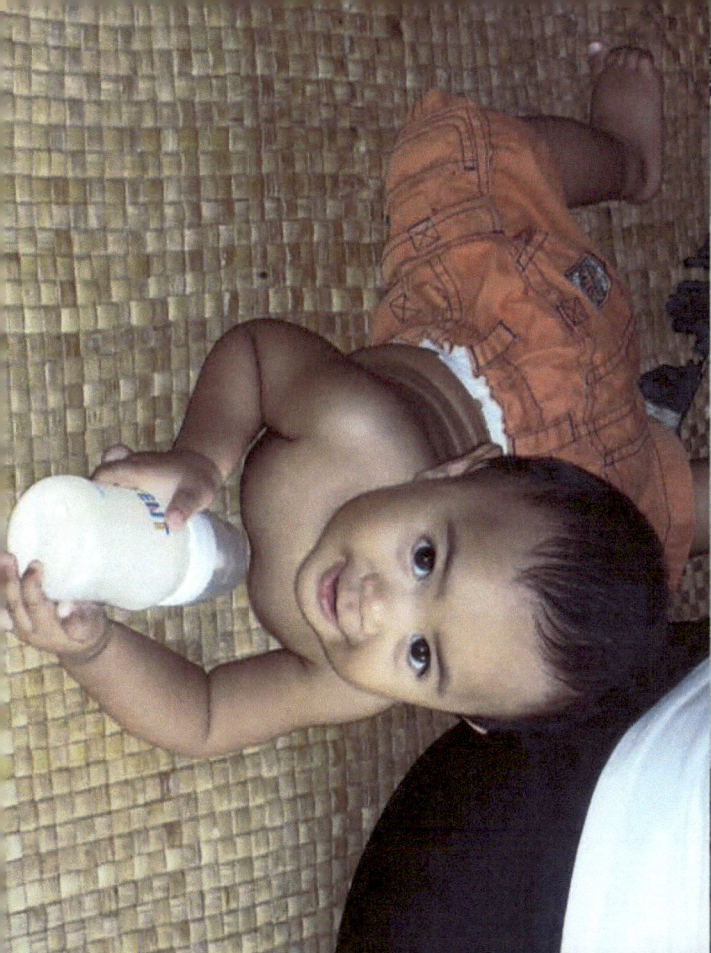

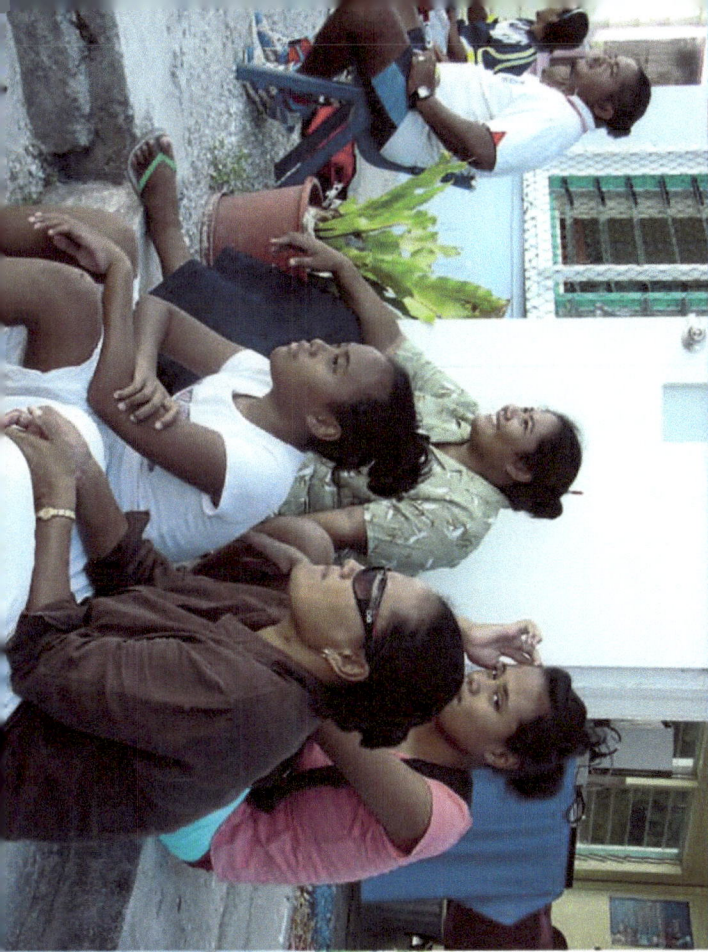

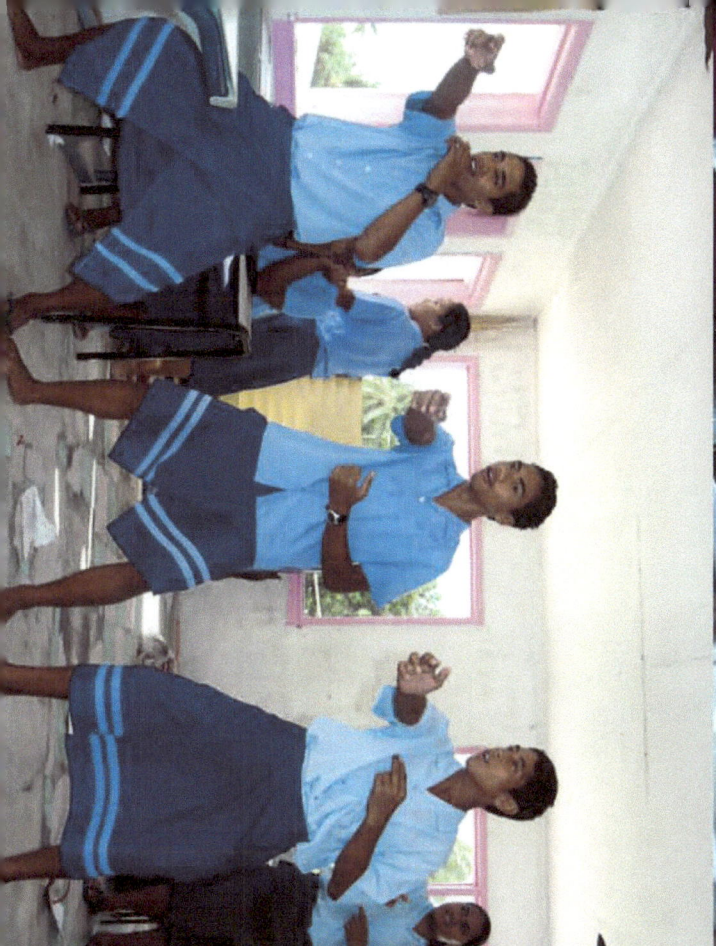